COLLECTION LATOMUS
VOLUME 169

RECRUITMENT
AND
THE PROGRAMME OF TIBERIUS GRACCHUS

D/1980/0415/86
ISBN 2-87031-109-5

COLLECTION LATOMUS
Fondée par Marcel RENARD
VOLUME 169

Yanir SHOCHAT

Recruitment and the Programme of Tiberius Gracchus

Published with the Help
of Haifa University, Israel

LATOMUS
REVUE D'ÉTUDES LATINES
60, RUE COLONEL CHALTIN
BRUXELLES
1980

To my dear parents

ACKNOWLEDGMENT

I wish to express my gratitude to Professor D. Ashery which under his guidance I wrote a work that was a cornerstone for this work. Many thanks to Prof. I. Schatzman, Prof. A. Gilboa, Prof. M. Amit and Prof. E. Gabba for their important remarks. I owe special thanks to Dr. M. Dagut for bringing the English into its present style.

CONTENTS

INTRODUCTION

The historian D. C. Earl writes as follows in his book about Tiberius Gracchus : "Now if Tiberius Gracchus' purpose was military and not primarily social, agrarian or economic, then this feature of his law does make sense. The legions were recruited from citizens with a certain property qualification and to increase the number of citizens available, the landless unemployed had to be supplied with the necessary qualification. And for this purpose it was vital that the allotments should be made inalienable" (1).

It is not my intention in this book to dispute Earl's point regarding whether the law was logical from a social point of view, or not. It is fairly clear that Tiberius' concern was not with economics, but with the social implications of the decline of the class of small farmers and the massing of a large proletariat in Rome. On this subject the opinion put forward by H. Last is far more convincing : "The business of Tiberius was to relieve the widespread unemployment of the urban population, and the plan he adopted to achieve this end was a scheme for the partial redistribution of the public land — a scheme so sane in its conception and so successful in its results that it is futile to charge its author either with reckless vote-catching or with utopian aspirations of unpractical ignorance" (2).

Although it is possible to disagree with this author regarding the extent to which the entire reform was successful, and despite the fact that its long-term effectiveness in the social sphere was minimal, it cannot be defined as futile, as Earl attempts to do. In essence, it was in accord with the Roman tradition of settling the landless in colonies (even though in this context colonies were not discussed) and distributing land through *assignatio uiritim*. Even though there was a change in the mood of the Roman populace, and the movement to the city was not merely the result of dispossession but was also due to the attraction of Rome itself, the plan was fundamentally logical, despite the difficulties that it encountered. On

(1) D. C. Earl, *Tiberius Gracchus*, Brussels, 1963 (*Collection Latomus*, LXVI), pp. 37-38.

(2) H. Last, *C.A.H.*, vol. IX, p. 89.

the other hand, Last's tendency to ignore the military aspect is unjustified, since there is no reason to reject Appian's account, which stresses this feature. In fact, not a few scholars (3) have accepted it as an integral part of Tiberius' reform, but not, in my opinion, correctly.

My object in this book is to demonstrate the error of the view that Tiberius' aim in distributing land was to increase the number of *assidui* who could be recruited for the legions. Although the reform had both a social and a military aspect, each of these related to a different category within the population. Tiberius' objective with regard to the Roman citizens was social rather than military, while the intention to distribute to the allies (4) derived primarily from his desire to increase the military burden upon them.

In the first two chapters of the book, I have attempted to show that there was no numerical shortage of *assidui* for recruitment purposes, while in the third chapter I have tried to demonstrate that the claim that Tiberius wanted to increase recruitment among the Roman citizens is unacceptable. On the contrary, he aspired to easing this burden by increasing recruitment among the allies. There can be no doubt that this thesis sheds new light on Tiberius' character as a statesman.

(3) A. E. ASTIN, *Scipio Aemilianus*, Oxford, 1967, p. 196 ; P. A. BRUNT, *Italian Manpower 225 B.C. - A.D. 14*, Oxford, 1971, p. 75 ; D. C. EARL, *op. cit.*, p. 34 ff. ; C. NICOLET, *Les Gracques ou crise agraire et révolution à Rome*, Paris, 1967, pp. 104-105 ; T. RICE HOLMES, *The Roman Republic and the Founder of the Empire*, Oxford, 1923, p. 15 ; H. H. SCULLARD, *From the Gracchi to Nero*, London, 1970, p. 23 ; A. J. TOYNBEE, *Hannibal's Legacy*, Oxford, 1965, vol. II, p. 96.

(4) On that subject see my article : *The lex agraria of 133 B.C. and the Italian Allies*, in *Athenaeum*, N.S. XLVIII (1970), p. 25 ff. and also BRUNT, *op. cit.*, p. 76, n. 1.

I

The Capite Censi and the Census Figures

The question of the inclusion of the *capite censi* in the census figures is of the utmost importance for understanding the nature of the military and social problems immediately prior to Tiberius Gracchus' appearance on the Roman political scene. Modern scholarship has frequently interpreted the difficulties of recruiting men for the legions at that time as being the result of a sharp demographic decline among the *assidui* (1).

However, if the census figures did not include the *capite censi*, there is no justification for referring to a sharp decline in the number of *assidui* and of consequent recruitment difficulties. This point is absolutely clear, for the lowest census figure recorded between the year 163/4 and that of Tiberius Gracchus' tribuneship was 317,933 (2). While the number of legions which existed at that time was between seven and eight (3), comprising less than 40,000 men (4). Since the soldiers constituted only one-eighth of the total number of those included in the census figure, the recruitment difficulties could not have been caused by the small number of *assidui*. Modern authorities have adduced a wide variety of arguments to prove that the *capite censi* were in fact included in the census figures. Beloch, the first to state this opinion, presented several arguments to support it (5). He posed the question : How is it possible that the phrase

(1) T. Rice Holmes, *The Roman Republic*, Oxford, 1923, vol. I, p. 15 ; K. B. Marsh, *A History of the Roman World from 146 to 30 B.C.*, London, 1953, p. 32 ; D. C. Earl, *Tiberius Gracchus*, Brussels, 1965 (*Collection Latomus*, LXVI), pp. 32-35 ; A. J. Toynbee, *Hannibal's Legacy*, Oxford, 1965, vol. II, pp. 92 and 96 ; H. H. Scullard, *From the Gracchi to Nero*, London, 1970, p. 23 ; P. A. Brunt, *Italian Manpower 225 B.C. - 14 A.D.*, Oxford, 1971, p. 75.

(2) Liv., *Per.*, lvi.

(3) P. A. Brunt, *op. cit.*, p. 432. He also holds that the average number of legions under arms was about 7 (p. 429).

(4) P. A. Brunt (*op. cit.*, p. 429) says that the average number of *assidui* serving in the legions was 35,000.

(5) *Die Bevölkerung der griechisch-römischen Welt*, Leipzig, 1886, p. 312 ff.

censa sunt capita ciuium tot contains any suggestion that the *capite censi* were not included in the census figures? (6) ("Wie könnten die capite censi in dem civium capita nicht einbegriffen sein?") (7). He also argued that in the period between 338 B.C. and 275 B.C. the population density in the *ager Romanus* was very great, precluding the possibility of the *capite censi* being excluded from the census figures (8). He queried whether at the time of the Second Punic War there could have been a shortage of soldiers, as indeed there was, if the last recorded census figures from before the War included only *assidui* (234/3 B.C. — 270,212)? (9) He was particularly anxious to show that there could not have been any increase in the census figure of the year 125 B.C. as a result of the activity of the *tres uiri a.d.a.i.* commission, since after the year 129 B.C. the activity of this commission came to a virtual end. In his opinion a mistake had crept into the census records for 125 B.C. and 115 B.C. and there had been no numerical increase at all. He claimed that the figure C had mistakenly been added to the two numbers, thus increasing their value by 100,000 (10).

Fraccaro, who accepted Beloch's argument (even claiming that he knew of no serious attempt to refute it), concentrated mainly on the problem of interpreting the census figure for 125 B.C. (11). He rejected Mommsen's opinion that the increase of 75.913 in this census was caused by the activity of the *III uiri agris dandis adsignandis iudicandis* commission, which was established for the implementation of the *lex Sempronia agraria* of 133 B.C. He contended that : 1) the land which was distributed was not *optimo iure e censui censendo*, i.e. the recipient of the land did not declare it to the censor, and therefore his status did not change from *capite census* to *assiduus*. Thus, the number of *assidui* did not necessarily increase as a result of this land distribution (12). 2) It is not clear why the activity of this commission was not felt by the time of the 131/0 census, which is not substantially larger than that of 136/5 B.C., exceeding it by only a few hundred. He argued that, if the census figures included only the *assidui*, and the land distribution changed the *capite censi* to *assidui*,

(6) *Op. cit.*, p. 318.
(7) *Klio*, vol. III (1903), p. 478.
(8) In *Bevölkerung*, p. 318.
(9) *Op. cit.*, p. 317.
(10) *Op. cit.*, pp. 351-352.
(11) *Assegnazioni agrarie e censimenti romani*, in *Opuscula*, II, Pavia, 1957, p. 87 ff.
(12) *Op. cit.*, pp. 87-88.

the increase should have been much larger, since the commission took energetic steps towards land distribution immediately after 133 B.C. Thus, the census of 125 B.C. does not attest to a numerical increase resulting from the *capite censui* becoming *assidui* (13). Fraccaro accepted Beloch's opinion that in reality there had been no increase but rather a decline in the 125 B.C. census figure, since he thought, like Beloch, that there had been a mistake in the manuscript and that a figure C had been added to the figure (14).

Toynbee does not contribute much to this discussion, stating only that from the words *proletarius* and *capite censi*, it can be inferred that the *capite censi* were numbered by the censor, for if a person was not a *pater familias* he had to declare himself a *caput*, i.e. by registering his name and the name of his tribe, if he had any sons, however, he had to declare his *proles* (15).

To these arguments P. A. Brunt (16) added that the very fact that the poorest section of the population was called *capite censi* shows that it was included in the census. He gave no explanation of this assertion, but most probably his point was that the word *censi*, which means "enumerated", indicated that they were counted and, having no possession to declare, they declared their *caput*. He also contended that the government had to know their number, since the *capite censi* served in the navy and, in times of emergency, the amount of money which was the minimum requirement for service in the legions was reduced or annulled so that they could enter its ranks. The *capite censi*, therefore, definitely fell into the category of *ciues qui arma ferre possent*. It was also necessary to include them in the censor's lists for the purposes of voting and division into tribes. Brunt's stand was partially based on the background to Tiberius Gracchus' tribuneship, as it has been interpreted by modern scholars. If the *assidui* alone were included in the census figures, Brunt maintained, there should not have been any grounds for the fear during the Gracchian period that there would be a dearth in manpower. He also claimed that the shortage of manpower among Roman citizens during the Civil War of 90/89 B.C., when the *proletarii* served regularly in the legions, shows that

(13) *Op. cit.*, p. 88. See also J. Kromayer, *Die wirtschaftliche Entwicklung Italiens im II. und I. Jahrhundert vor Chr.*, in *Neue Jahrbücher*, 17. Jahrgang (1914), pp. 157-158 and p. 158, n. 2 ; and J. Göhler, *Rom und Italien*, Breslau, 1939, pp. 139-140.

(14) *Op. cit.*, pp. 90-91 and 100-101.

(15) *Op. cit.*, pp. 464-465.

(16) *Op. cit.*, pp. 22-25.

the total number of citizens was not much larger than the figure given at the end of the 2nd century B.C.

Despite these arguments in favour of the thesis outlined above, in my opinion it has not been conclusively proved that the *capite censi* were included in the census figures. Some of the arguments lack any real validity, while, as regards the key question — the connection between the land distribution and the increase in the 125 B.C. census figure — all of the many efforts devoted to disproving this, have, in my opinion, been completely unsuccessful. Neither has any solid basis been established for the thesis that not only was there no increase but, in fact, a decline in the total number. I believe that an additional connection may be found between the distribution of land among Roman citizens in *ager Gallicus et Picenus* in the year 232 B.C. and the possible increase in the figures recorded in censuses held after this date and before the Second Punic War. In both cases, viz. in consequence of both the land distribution of 232 B.C. and of that implemented by the Gracchan commission, the propertyless citizens who had previously not been included in the census figures became *assidui*, were then included in the census and caused an increase in the figures. It is true that some of the arguments show that it was necessary to ascertain the number of propertyless persons, and it is therefore very probable that they were counted, but there is no evidence that they were included in the census figures. They may well have been numbered separately, as may be inferred from analogies with other groups of people for whom this was true. Since, in my opinion, the arguments for considering that the *capite censi* were not included in the census figures are more convincing than the above, the overall problem will be discussed below, beginning with claims which do not succeed in proving anything about the manner in which the *capite censi* were registered. This will be followed by an attempt to show that the *capite censi* were not included in the census figures.

As stated above, the formula *censa sunt capita ciuium* served as a basis for the assumption that propertyless persons were included in the census figures. However, the phrasing of this formula, which is frequently used by Livy (whenever he mentions the results of the censuses) [17] makes it clear only that those persons who were not Roman citizens were not

(17) Livius, III, 3, 9 ; III, 24, 10 ; *Per.* X ; *Per.* XIII ; *Per.* XIV ; *Per.* XVIII ; *Per.* XIX ; *Per.* XX ; XXVII, 36, 7 ; *Per.* XXVII ; *Per.* XXIX ; XXXV, 9, 2 ; XXXVIII, 36, 10 ; *Per.* XXXVIII ; *Per.* XLII ; XLII, 10, 2 ; *Per.* XLV ; *Per.* XLVI ; *Per.* XLVII ; *Per.* XLVIII ; *Per.* LIV ; *Per.* LVI ; *Per.* LIX ; *Per.* LX ; *Per.* LXIII.

included in the figures. Thus, the figures included only Roman citizens — *capita ciuium* — but this does not necessarily mean that they included all categories of citizens. In this connection it might be worthwhile to examine the status of *ciues sine suffragio*.

Ciues sine suffragio were Roman citizens of inferior status who had no political rights. From a legal point of view they could be included in the category of *capita ciuium*, but were they also included in the census figure? Many scholars maintain that they were [18], the main argument being that they served in the legions. I see no reason to disagree with Festus' [19] statement that the *municipes sine suffragio* served in the legions, but their number could have been known from separate registration lists for recruitment, which need not have been included in the census figures. Indeed, there are grounds for this view. It is highly probable that they were not numbered at Rome, but in their own municipalities and by censors of their own [20]. The census figures may have been sent to Rome [21] ; however, even if this were the case, as I tend to think, it may be assumed that there was a separate register for them. There is no evidence that they were in any way included in the census figures. On the other hand, it may be inferred that those included in the *tabulae caeritium* appeared only on a separate register.

These registers included those citizens of the municipium of Caere who were *ciues sine suffragio*, and Roman citizens who had been deprived of their voting rights by the censors as a form of punishment [22], becoming in effect *ciues sine suffragio*. Thus, the lists contained only *ciues sine suffragio*, but we cannot be sure that they contained all the *ciues sine suffragio*. The argument advanced for the assumption that all those holding partial citizenship were included in the lists is that Caere was the first municipium to obtain partial citizenship, and that therefore all additional citizens holding such citizenship as a result of the granting of this status to new municipia were entered in its lists [23]. This assumption

(18) Beloch, *Bevölkerung*, p. 319 ; E. T. Salmon, *Roman Colonization from the Second Punic War to the Gracchi*, in *J.R.S.*, vol. XXVI (1936), p. 16, n. 88 ; E. Gabba, *Ancora sulle cifre dei censimenti*, in *Athenaeum*, vol. XL (N.S. XXX) (1952), p. 170 ; Toynbee, *op. cit.*, p. 456 ; Brunt, *op. cit.*, p. 16 ff.

(19) L. 126, L. 117, L. 155.

(20) *C.I.L.*, XI, n. 3616, 3617 ; Toynbee, *op. cit.*, pp. 210 and 220 ; Brunt, *op. cit.*, p. 19.

(21) Toynbee, *op. cit.*, pp. 220-221.

(22) Strabo, V, 2, 3 ; Gellius, XVI, 13, 7.

(23) This possible argument is brought by Brunt, *op. cit.*, p. 515.

does not hold for two reasons : 1) Even had Caere been the first municipium to receive this status, it seems improbable that the lists of citizens from a metropolis like Capua would have been included in those of a small town. 2) Brunt has shown that Caere was not the first municipium *sine suffragio* but, on the contrary, the last (24). Thus, if the Caere lists did not in fact include all the *ciues sine suffragio*, Brunt is correct in stating that (25) other municipia had separate lists of citizens similar to this. In any case, it is important to note that the *tabulae caeritum* are an example of the registration of *ciues sine suffragio*, even if they contained only the citizens of Caere and the Roman citizens who had been punished. The Caere register is instructive, as can be learned from the following passage from Strabo (26) : *οἱ μὲν οὖν Ῥωμαῖοι ... οὐχ ἱκανῶς ἀπομνημονεῦσαι τὴν χάριν αὐτοῖς δοκοῦσι. πολιτείαν γὰρ δόντες οὐκ ἀνέγραψαν εἰς τοὺς πολίτας, ἀλλὰ καὶ τοὺς ἄλλους τοὺς μὴ μετέχοντας τῆς ἰσονομίας εἰς τὰς δέλτους ἐξώριζον τὰς καιρετανῶν.* The ingratitude of the Romans towards the inhabitants of Caere, which finds expression in this quotation, lay not in the nature of the rights of Roman citizenship which had been conferred on them, but in the fact that they had not been registered as part of the body of Roman citizenry : *πολιτείαν γὰρ δόντες οὐκ ἀνέγραψαν εἰς τοὺς πολίτας*. The rest of the passage also indicates that Strabo was troubled by the registration, for he states that those who took no part in *ἰσονομία* were removed or banished *ἐξώριζον* to the list where the Caereans were registered. It is only logical that if the citizens of Caere belonged by registration to the body of citizenry, but were enumerated separately in the general list, they would not have been able to regard this as a sign of discrimination or ingratitude. On the contrary, it would have been natural for a certain municipal entity to be registered separately within the general list. Therefore, since ingratitude is mentioned, it is clear that something more important — their classification as foreigners — is involved. It is not so significant that additional persons were included in the *tabulae caeritum*. It may therefore be concluded that they were removed from the lists of Roman citizens. The formula, *censa sunt capita ciuium*, does not refer to them and, consequently, does not designate any of the inhabitants of the municipia *sine suffragio*, for there was certainly no special reason to discriminate against the people of Caere.

(24) Brunt, *op. cit.*, p. 515 ff.
(25) *Op. cit.*, p. 20.
(26) V, 2, 3.

As will be demonstrated below, there is strong evidence to support the thesis that the Roman manpower figures cited by Polybius for 225 B.C. are greater by 55,000 than the census figure for the year 234/3, the last recorded figure from before 225 B.C. Polybius notes that the Roman manpower figures which he cites also include Campanians (27). Indeed, it would be difficult to explain this steep increase without assuming that Polybius had added the number of Campanians to the total figure. This proves that the people of Campania, i.e. Capua, were not included in the census figures. It is possible that the census figure for the year 189/8, or perhaps 179/8, supports the assumption that the *ciues sine suffragio* were not included in the census figures. There are signs that in 189 B.C. the process of restoring the status of *ciuitas sine suffragio* to Capua was begun : Capua had been deprived of this status as a result of its betrayal of Rome at the time of the Second Punic War. In that year the inhabitants of Capua were first numbered and it was decided that this would take place at Rome. A year later they were awarded the *ius connubii* (28). It is reasonable to suppose that the act of being numbered signified the end of the state of *deditio* of the Capuans. The conferring of the *ius connubii* indicates that they were given civil rights which were awarded to *ciuitates sine suffragio*. It is possible that in 188, when Arpinum, Formiae, and Fundi were granted the status of *ciuitas optimo iure*, the status of *ciuitas sine suffragio* was awarded to Capua (29). Therefore, if the population of a city with partial citizenship had been included in the census figure, the restitution of this status to Capua should have been reflected in the figure of the census taken after this event. The number of inhabitants of Capua can be estimated as having been at least 30,000, since in 216 B.C. the number of *iuniores* was 34,000 (30). To this figure the *seniores* should be added, and from it those killed during the Second Punic War or banished permanently in 211 should be subtracted. There should have been a corresponding rise in the census figure. However, the census figure for 189/8 rose by only 14,614 (31), whereas that for 179/8 exceeded that of

(27) II, 24.

(28) Livius, XXXVIII, 36, 5-6.

(29) There is no evidence in the sources for Toynbee's assumption that at Capua there was administrative vacuum till 59 B.C. See *op. cit.*, I, p. 224.

(30) Livius, XXIII, 5, 15.

(31) We must accept the amendment of the number of the *capita ciuium* — 243,704 concerning the census of 194/3. In Livius, XXXV, 9, there appears the number 143,704. The number of *capita ciuium* in census 189/8 was 258,318 (Livius, XXXVIII, 36).

189/8 by only a few hundred (32). If partial citizenship was indeed conferred upon Capua, this is not reflected in the census figure.

On the other hand, it is likely that the 189/8 census reflects the bestowal of *ciuitas optimo iure* status on Arpinum, Formiae, and Fundi (33), which were small cities. As a result of their new status, the inhabitants were included in the census figure and caused it to increase. Brunt confidently states that, if the Campanians (meaning the Capuans) had not been included in the figure, Polybius would certainly have given their number separately and would not have added them to the Romans in his survey of Roman and Italian manpower in the year 225 B.C. (34). However, this does not constitute serious evidence for their being included in the figure, as it can be interpreted differently. In undertaking his survey, Polybius may have made a distinction between the manpower potential for legion service and that for the auxiliary force. The Campanians, who served in the legions, are mentioned in conjunction with the Romans, whereas other peoples, who served in the auxiliary force, are listed separately. There may have been an additional, bureaucratic reason for the Campanians' being mentioned together with the Romans. Manpower statistics from the allies were obtained, as Polybius explicitly states, as the result of a specific demand sent from Rome in 225 B.C. (35) ; whereas the statistics from Capua were already in the possession of the censors, since they were sent to Rome regularly after every census there. These statistics were part of the records kept by the censorial bureaucracy, which was not the case as regards the manpower statistics from the allies. The figures for the Sabines, who were at that time probably *ciues optimo iure*, appear together with those of the Etruscans, but separately from the Romans. This, however, appears to have been the result of the fact that this military force was recruited by the *tumultus* system (36), i.e. in great haste and not by census lists.

Formally and in terms of civil rights, the *capite censi* ranked above the *ciues sine suffragio*, since they had political rights. In fact, however, the aristocratic government treated them as an inferior class. They were not called the sixth class but *infra classem* and, because of the contempt in

(32) The number of *capita ciuium* in census 179/8 was 258,794 (Livius, *Per.* XLI).

(33) Livius, XXXVIII, 36, 7.

(34) *Op. cit.*, p. 20.

(35) II, 23, 9.

(36) II, 24, 5. The basis to this indication are the words ἐκ τοῦ καιροῦ. See A. Afzelius, *Die römische Eroberung Italiens (340-264 v.Chr.)*, Kobenhavn, 1942, pp. 101-102 ; Toynbee, *op. cit.*, I, p. 480.

which they were held, they were only accorded one *centuria* in the *comitia centuriata*. The authorities were less interested in their number than in that of the *ciues sine suffragio*, since they neither served in the legions or paid taxes to the Roman treasury. It is therefore probable that their registration was undertaken in a way similar to that of the *ciues sine suffragio*. Just as the formula *censa sunt capita ciuium* implies nothing as regards the manner in which the *ciues sine suffragio* were registered, it is equally meaningless concerning the propertyless class. Moreover, the additional phrase contained in the formula — *praeter orbos orbasque* (Liv., III, 39) or *praeter pupillos pupillas* (Liv., Ept. LIX), which is usually regarded as an indication of the registration procedure (37) — implies that children who had parents, and married women, were also included in the figure. However, since this is known not to have been the case, no conclusions regarding the composition of the total figure can be drawn from the phrasing of the formula.

Beloch's argument that the high population density of the *ager Romanus* between the years 338 and 275 seems to indicate that the *capite censi* were included in the figure is very weak, both because of the worthlessness of an argument of this kind and because the data in our possession provide no confirmation of the thesis that the population density was indeed great.

If we suppose that the population density in the *ager Romanus* was actually high in comparison with that of other nations at the time, it may well have been greater than that implied by the census figure. Furthermore, since there is no precise data concerning the number of *capite censi* at the time, their number may have been small ; in which case, its influence on population density would have been minimal. It is, therefore, pointless to make this the basis for an argument concerning whether or not the *capite censi* were included in the census figure. The truth of the matter is that we do not know very much about the population density in the *ager Romanus*, for it is unclear whether the census figures up to 264 B.C., and perhaps even up to 240 B.C., have any validity. Brunt has shown that the fluctuations in the census figures before that year are not compatible with other events of the same period and he suggests that we treat them sceptically (38). To illustrate Brunt's argument,

(37) Beloch, *Bevölkerung*, p. 308 ; Gabba, *Origini dell'esercito professionale in Roma*, in *Athenaeum*, N.S. XXVII (1949), p. 189 ; Toynbee, *op. cit.*, p. 463.

(38) *Op. cit.*, p. 32, he says : "In sum it is impossible to affirm or deny with certainty that the census figures between 339 and 263 are authentic, but we can be sure that if they

I will adduce one very striking example. Orosius tells us (39) that, in the 481st year after the founding of Rome (266 B.C.) (40), a severe epidemic broke out, lasting two years. The deaths it caused were so numerous that in the census figures, according to Orosius, it was not the number of deaths which were noted, but the number of those who remained alive. Although this is an exaggeration, the official census figure gives no sign that there was an epidemic. The census figure for 265/4 is 292,334 (41) whereas for 276/5, the year of the latest census before this of which we have records, the total was 271,224 (42). Thus, not only had the figure not decreased, but it had actually increased by about 21,000. Clearly this increase is unrealistic. Moreover, in the period between 338 and 290 B.C., the *ager Romanus* grew by 150%. A large portion of the annexed territory was empty and suitable for settlement by citizens (43). It is therefore unreasonable to state that the population density in the *ager Romanus* at that time was high.

The background to Tiberius Gracchus' appearance on the political scene, as interpreted by modern scholars, supports the contentions of those scholars who maintain that the *capite censi* were included in the census figure. Astin, who is inclined to think that the *capite censi* were included in this figures, writes (44) :

"The recorded census figures of the second century show a general rise up to 164 and thereafter ... decline until 136... It shows a decline of nearly 6 per cent over 18 years. If this is the decline in the numbers of the class available for the levy, while it does not represent a catastrophic collapse, it is quite sufficient to have caused serious concern especially ... that it was likely to continue. But if, as

are, those for 339 and 293 stand in an implausible chronological connection with other events, and that the traditional dating is probably at fault..., the doubts about the authenticity of the figures before 264 must extend to those between 264 and 240". And on p. 33 : "It therefore seems best ... to be sceptical of the authenticity of all the figures down to the first Punic War at earliest".

(39) IV, 5.

(40) Orosius says that the pestilence broke out in the four hundred and eighty first year after the founding of the city. In regular counting, taking 753 as the year of the foundation of Rome, that means 272 B.C. But since he says that the first Punic War started in the four hundredth and eighty third year after the founding of Rome (IV, 7), it is obvious that the starting year for Orosius' dating was not 753 and the pestilence broke out in 266 and not in 272 B.C.

(41) Eutropius, II, 18. In Livius, *Per.* XVI the number is 382,234, but surely this is a mistake and it should be 282,234. Nevertheless it indicates a rise of 11,000.

(42) Livius, *Per.* XIV.

(43) Brunt, *op. cit.*, p. 31.

(44) *Scipio Aemilianus*, Oxford, 1967, pp. 337-338.

seems more probable, this is a decline in the total male citizen population, the position was even more alarming ... if the *civium capita* are the entire male citizen population, the declining total shown by the census figures indicates a low birth-rate and this corresponds to the evidence of Appian and Plutarch who both state that the poor were neglecting the rearing of children, and to the implication of the speech of Metellus Macedonicus in which he urged the people to marry in order to beget children... Finally, the largest single drop was evidently revealed by the census of 136. The difference since 142 was 10.509, more than half the total decline since 164 ... if the figure is correct it is likely to have come as a shock, especially as the previous census had shown the only rise since 164."

Astin, who is much more cautious in his phrasing than Brunt, presents arguments that help to refute his own opinion. He himself states that even if the figure includes only the *assidui*, the decline evidenced "is quite sufficient to have caused serious concern especially ... that it was likely to continue". The downward trend gave cause for concern, especially since in 136 B.C. the most drastic decline since 164 was recorded. Astin states : "It is likely to have come as a shock, especially as the previous census had shown the only rise since 164". From this passage it is quite clear that he well understood that, even if the *capite censi* were not included in the census figure, there was cause for concern in Rome. On the other hand, he is far from convincing when he claims that if the *capite censi* were included in the figure, then the decline of 136/5 reflects a decline in natural increase, as is mentioned by Appian and Plutarch and which, according to Astin, is indicated in the speech by Metellus Macedonicus, the censor of 131 B.C. In this connection, we should ask, therefore, which interpretation of the 136/5 census figure seems more probable — a decline in the natural increase caused by a low birth-rate and high infant death-rate, or the fact that the *assidui* became *capite censi*? It is absolutely certain that children under the age of 17 were not included in the census figure. From Astin's argument it transpires, therefore, that between 157 and 152 B.C. there was a lower birth-rate and higher infant death-rate than in the five preceding years. However, we have no data which can explain why these two phenomena should have occurred precisely in those years. There is no evidence to show that dispossession of the poor and the population shift to the city in those years were significantly greater than in the five preceding years. There is also no evidence to support the theory that urban residence during this period caused a sharp decline in natural increase. Boren (45), who has proved that employment

(45) *The Urban Side of the Gracchan Economic Crisis*, in *AHR*, 63 (1958), p. 890 ff.

was available in Rome until 140 B.C., has supplied information supporting the contention that there was no such decline. Moreover, it should follow from Astin's argument that during the following five years, from 152 to 147, the decline in natural increase came to a halt, but there is no apparent explanation for this. On the contrary, it is probable that during those years dispossession and the mass movement to the city intensified, accompanied by a decline in the birth-rate. The census figure for the year 131/0, however, showed a growth of a few hundred in comparison with the previous census. One item of information enables us to connect the decline in the census figure of 136/5 with the reduction in the number of *assidui*. Boren has shown that, due to the diminished flow of money to Rome, building and public works were stopped after 140 and the number of those unemployed grew. Since the minimum property requirement for being counted in the ranks of the *assidui* was 4,000 asses, a sum whose purchasing power was very low (a year's supply of prepared bread for four people (46), or one year's rent for very humble living quarters) (47), it is reasonable to suppose that those employed on public works were *assidui* who, when unemployed, became *capite censi*. It is very probable that it was this and not the drop in the birth-rate, which accounted for the decline in the census figure of 136/5 B.C. The census figure of 131/0 rose by a few hundred, due to the work of the *tresuiri* in distributing land, the effects of which had begun to influence the conversion of *capite censi* into *assidui*.

It is necessary to examine Brunt's argument that if the census figure included only the *assidui* it would be difficult to understand the fear of a decline in manpower which was felt prior to the Gracchan period. My concern here is not with the recruitment difficulties encountered on the eve of Tiberius Gracchus' tribunate (which will be discussed in the next chapter) but only with the information available concerning the population decline and the influence this had on military manpower. Appian is the only source to explicitly connect the demographic decline with the fear of a shortage of military manpower (48). However he was certainly referring to the allies rather than to the Roman citizens. His

(46) It is known that one person's consumption was 60 *modii* of wheat per year. That means more than 600 *asses*. Baked bread obviously cost more and it would not be far off the mark to estimate it at a minimum of 1,000 *asses* per year.

(47) Plutarch tells that Sulla, when he was young and poor, paid 3,000 sesterts as rent. A freedman paid 2,000 sesterts as rent for an upper chamber in the same building (*Sulla*, 1).

(48) *B.C.*, I, 7-8.

remarks on this subject are clear and do not leave much room for doubt. He writes that after the conquest of Italy, the Romans divided the land among the allies so that they might increase in numbers. The process of dispossession from the land had caused their decline, arousing the concern of the *δῆμος*, i.e. the Roman people, who feared they would not have many allies. The attempt to prevent this by legislation aimed at limiting the area of land held by private individuals failed. T. Gracchus' appearance on the political scene came as a result of the continued impoverishment and numerical decline of the allies. In describing the background to the appearance of Tiberius Gracchus, Appian makes no mention of the decline in the number of Roman citizens. He stresses that it was the body of Roman citizens that was concerned about a possible lack of allies, and does not even hint at any concern among the authorities regarding the decline in the number of Roman citizens. The attempt to maintain that Appian used the term "allies" to mean Roman citizens is devoid of any factual basis [49].

Plutarch, whose work also contains a reference to the demographic problem, is less clear than Appian on this matter. He writes that a decline in the number of freemen was felt throughout Italy, but he is careful not to state that this decline was felt among Roman citizens despite that he later stresses that they were dispossessed of their land [50]. I have shown elsewhere [51] that it is reasonable to suppose that Appian and Plutarch relied on a common source which, in describing the background to the appearance of Tiberius Gracchus, stressed the pan-Italic military aspect and connected the demographic-military problem with the allies. I have also shown there that, even if Plutarch and Appian did not have a common source, Plutarch's source emphasised this aspect and influenced him in his description of the background to Tiberius Gracchus' tribuneship. For us it is important to note that, in describing the Tiberius Gracchus affair itself, Plutarch makes no mention whatsoever of the demographic decline among the Roman citizens, merely stating that Tiberius wished to solve a social problem (not a demographic-military one) among the Roman citizens. He does not refer to the allies at all. Thus, in describing Tiberius' tribunate, Plutarch deviated from the pan-Italic approach, which stressed the demographic-military problem among the allies, and concentrated on the Roman socio-economic aspect of the

(49) See my article, *Athenaeum*, N.S. XLVIII (1970), p. 40 ff.
(50) *Tiberius Gracchus*, 8.
(51) *Op. cit.*, p. 34 ff.

matter. In short, Appian dealt with the shortage of manpower among the allies rather than among the Roman citizens, whereas Plutarch referred briefly, without going into detail, to the decline of the freemen throughout Italy as opposed to the increase in slaves. His approach clearly reflected the pan-Italic conception which had nothing to do with Roman citizens.

Those passages in the sources which refer to the speech about marriage and procreation made by Q. Metellus Macedonicus in the year 131, when he was a censor, do not mention any shortage of military manpower nor do they refer to any anxiety on that point. A detailed analysis of the sources, and a discussion of the thesis that the censor's speech does not support the theory that there was a lack of *assidui*, will be given in the next chapter. The fact that the problem of recruitment did not stem from a dearth of *assidui* may be deduced from the fact that manpower problems existed at the time of the Civil War too, when the proletariat served in the legions. Appian states that it was necessary to draft *Libertini* because of the shortage of soldiers [52]. Even if Brunt's high numerical estimate [53] of 175,000 men drafted by Rome at the time of the Civil War, including citizens who received their citizenship during that period, is correct, it is clear that even at the most critical period of its history Rome was able to call up less than a half of its manpower. The 115 B.C. census, the last extant from before the war, lists close to 400,000 persons [54], from which it may be concluded that there were many draft evaders and that many people evidently never received their recruitment orders. Be that as it may, the fact that difficulties were encountered in recruiting forces for this war does not necessarily imply that the *capite censi* were included in the census figure. If approximately 200,000 men were not recruited, then certainly the Roman government's control of the manpower reservior was faulty in the extreme. It may well be, therefore, that the number of citizens not drafted was far greater than the discrepancy between the census figure and the number of soldiers recruited.

We may give an affirmative answer to Beloch's rhetorical question, whether it was possible for a shortage of soldiers to be created at the time of the Second Punic War, if the census figure included only *assidui*. Although it may not be possible to say that Beloch's argument is without any value, it can be shown that it is far from convincing, even if at first glance it may appear to be so. Here are some facts and figures to show

(52) App., *B.C.* , I, 49.
(53) *Op. cit.*, p. 439.
(54) The census figure of that year is 394,336 (Liv., *Per.* LXIII).

what Beloch's view really means. The total for the last extant census before the Punic War, held in 234/3, is 270,212 (55). Judging from the upward trend of the previous census figures (56), it is reasonable to suppose that, on the eve of the war, the number had risen to about 300,000. In the year 214 B.C. the censors checked their lists and found that only 2,000 *iuniores* were illegally evading service in the army (57). In that year there were 20 legions (58), two of them consisting of *uolones*. This means that about 90,000 Roman citizens were recruited (59), representing the total Roman manpower available to the legions at that time.

There is therefore, a discrepancy of more than 200,000 between the expected total on the eve of the Second Punic War and the actual number of men who constituted Roman manpower. In Beloch's opinion, this discrepancy can be explained only if the *capite censi* were included in the census figures (60). This however, is not the case. The discrepancy can be reduced, or even eliminated, when the following categories are taken into consideration : 1. *seniores* ; 2. soldiers who had completed their service by 214 B.C. and were legally exempt from service ; 3. the sick and others who were exempt from service because they were priests, officials, orderlies, maritime colonists, or for other reasons (61) ; 4. the great losses before the year 214 B.C. ; 5. *assidui* serving with the navy. Let us consider each one of these separately.

1. *Seniores*. As we have no way of estimating the average life-expectancy in Italy at that time, any figure would be mere guesswork. Comparisons with the Italian agricultural population at a later period may provide us with a rough idea, but are not to be regarded as trustworthy. We will content ourselves with citing modern hypotheses concerning the ratio of *seniores* to *iuniores*. Beloch's estimate (62) that the ratio was 1 : 2

(55) Liv., *Per.* XX.

(56) The census figure of the year 241/0 is 260,000 (Liv., *Per.* XIX). The rise in the next figure is about 10,000 men.

(57) Liv., XXIV, 18, 7-8.

(58) See Toynbee, *op. cit.*, II, pp. 64-67 ; Brunt, *op. cit.*, p. 418.

(59) From Brunt, *op. cit.*, p. 66, it is understood that the recruitment of six new legions was performed after the censors had checked their lists, and was made possible because of the reduction in property qualifications for legionary service. To the new legions *capite censi* were recruited. But Livius indicates the fact of the recruitment before his narration about the checking of the lists by the censors (Liv., XXIV, 11, 4-6).

(60) *Bevölkerung*, p. 377.

(61) See Brunt, *op. cit.*, p. 391, n. 1.

(62) *Bevölkerung*, p. 362.

seems improbable, since it would imply that the average life-expectancy was 60, which would be too high. Afzelius maintains (63) that the ratio was 1 : 3. Brunt accepts this (64) with certain reservations, considering it to be rather on the low side. He estimates that there were more than 3 *iuniores* to every *senior* (65).

2. It is impossible to estimate the number of soldiers who had completed their service by 214 B.C., for the following reasons :

a. We are not sure of the legal length of service (the term of 16 years mentioned by Polybius is an emendation made by later editors) ;

b. We have no exact knowledge regarding the recruitment policy between the two Punic Wars. Neither do we know whether the object of this policy was to force the soldiers to finish their term of service, i.e. to base the army on veteran soldiers, or to recruit all the citizens, thus reducing military service for all and creating a situation where only a few soldiers completed the legally permitted quota of years.

3. It is difficult to ascertain the precise number of legions between the two wars. It seems probable that, since military activity was more limited than during the second century B.C., the average number of legions was smaller.

4. We have no knowledge whatsoever about the number of men exempt from service because of illness or for other reasons. There is some basis for the supposition that between the First and the Second Punic Wars there were plagues or other less serious epidemics which undermined the health of the Roman populace. Orosius reports (66) that a pestilence which broke out in Rome in 266 B.C. lasted for two years. Livy (67) mentions a plague which broke out in Rome and its environs in 208 B.C. Orosius also records (68) a conflagration and a flood which seriously affected Rome in 241 B.C. It can therefore be assumed that the epidemics or lesser calamities which struck the population between the two wars diminished the military manpower potential, and that the census figure included many who were unfit for military service.

5. There are estimates of civilian losses during the Second Punic War,

(63) *Die römische Eroberung Italiens (340-264 v.Chr.)*, Cobenhavn, 1942, p. 100.
(64) *Op. cit.*, p. 54.
(65) *Op. cit.*, p. 53, n. 2.
(66) IV, 5.
(67) Liv., XXVII, 23.
(68) IV, 11.

up to the year 214 B.C. Brunt, arguing that the number of dead given in the sources is exaggerated, estimates that 50,000 Roman citizens had been killed by 214 B.C. (69). A similar number is suggested by Toynbee's study (70).

6. The number of *assidui* serving in the navy and not in the legions is not known.

We see, therefore, that there are several factors which can account for the discrepancy, and may actually have done so. However, since their numerical significance is not clear there is no sense in performing arithmetical exercises to show how this was possible.

Several sources maintain that the census figure included all those who could bear arms. In discussing the first census, held by Servius Tullius, Livy writes : *Adicit scriptorum antiquissimus Fabius Pictor eorum qui arma ferre possent eum numerum fuisse* (71). Even though this statement is made only here, and is not repeated in reference to other censuses, Dionysius Halicarnassus maintains that the figure was : *ἀριθμὸς τῶν ἐχώντων τὴν στρατεύσιμον ἐλῖκιαν* (72) and Polybius, in rounding off his survey of Roman and Italian manpower in 225 B.C., states that the figure he quotes includes : *τῶν δυναμένων ὅπλα βαστάζειν* (73). In order to understand the meaning of these statements, we have to examine the following questions : a. Who are meant by the phrase *Qui arma ferre possent*? b. Were the *capite censi* included for census purposes in the category of those who were able to bear arms? c. What can be learned from the manpower survey of the year 225 B.C. recorded by Polybius, as regards whether the *capite censi* were included in the category of those able to bear arms and in the census figure?

E. Gabba maintains that the phrase *Qui arma ferre possent* is not to be taken literally. He claims that it does not refer to those who could bear arms because they were healthy, since the medical rating of a Roman citizen was determined at the time of the *dilectus* and not by the censors during the census (74). I agree with Gabba for an additional reason. The census was held not only for military purposes, but also in order to decide

(69) *Op. cit.*, pp. 419-420.
(70) *Op. cit.*, II, p. 66 ff.
(71) I, 44.
(72) XI, 63.
(73) II, 24, 16.
(74) *Le origini dell'esercito professionale in Roma*, in *Athenaeum*, N.S. XXVII, 1949, p. 188.

on the *tributum*, to divide the property owners into five classes and to decide the *tribus* of every Roman citizen. If the sick were not included in the figure, this would mean that they were not included for tax purposes, class division, and tribal affiliation. This would not be logical. Therefore, since the phrase *Qui arma ferre possent* does not specifically designate healthy men but another category of citizens, probably a class whose members were termed "bearers of arms" as Gabba has noted, the question whether the *capite censi* belonged to this category or not must be examined. Brunt maintains that this was so, and that they were included amongst those *Qui arma ferre possent* and were therefore included in the census figure. It is, however, a moot point whether they came under the heading of those able to bear arms as far as the censor was concerned. It seems clear that in normal times they were not recruited to the legions, but did they serve in the navy as soldiers or were they recruited to the legions in times of crisis? Regarding service in the navy, it should be noted that before the First Punic War the Roman navy was very small, if it existed at all. It is therefore impossible to contend that the *capite censi* served in it before that war. At the beginning of the First Punic War, however, Rome established a large navy and many of the *capite censi* were recruited into it. If service in the navy is regarded as a basis for the argument that people without property were considered *Qui arma ferre possent*, it must be borne in mind that this does not hold good for the period prior to the First Punic War, and it must be assumed that, once the *capite censi* became *Qui arma ferre possent*, there would have been a change in the guiding principles of the census so as to include them in it. This may well have happened, but there is no extant evidence whatsoever to prove it. Polybius, who drew attention to the fact that the *capite censi* served in the navy [75], did not specify what the nature of their service was, whether they were employed as oarsmen, sailors or soldiers. Thiel's argument that in every *quinquereme* there were 40 *capite censi* serving as soldiers has no supporting evidence at all [76]. His claim is based on the assumption that there was a permanent guard on the ships, but we do not know anything about its existence, let alone its composition. If such a guard did in fact exist, there may have been some sort of arrangement for assigning legionaries to this duty, despite the fact that serving in the navy

(75) VI, 19.

(76) See *A History of Roman Sea-Power before the Second Punic War*, Amsterdam, 1954, pp. 77-78 ; also *Studies on the History of Roman Seapower in Republican Times*, Amsterdam, 1946, p. 196.

was less prestigious than serving in the infantry. This appears likely, both in view of the Roman practice of placing legionaries on ships during sea battles, and also because of the existence of the *legio classica*, which is an enigma to us [77]. It is possible that this legion consisted of contingents from the navy, but by the same token this could have been the permanent guard stationed on the ships, if such existed. In my opinion, service in the navy cannot be taken as solid proof that the *capite censi* were considered *Qui arma ferre possent*, since it may well have been that they did not bear arms but were oarsmen [78].

The contention that in times of crisis the propertyless classes were recruited to the legions needs examination and clarification. It is true that during the Pyrrhic War they served in the army. This is mentioned by Orosius [79], Augustinus [80], and Cassius Hemina [81], and Ennius too can be understood to refer to the recruitment of the *proletarii* in this war and no other [82]. From the fragment of Hemina it may be inferred that before 280 B.C. the *proletarii* were not recruited to the army, since he states that at that date, they were recruited for the first time. From this phrasing it may be concluded that the *proletarii* were recruited afterwards as well, but what we have to clarify is whether this was indeed so or whether their mobilization at the time of the Pyrrhic War was a unique event.

The point of departure for the discussion is the fact that there are four references to the service of the *proletarii* in the army during the Pyrrhic War, but not a single one relating to their service in a later war. Similarly, there is no reference to any particular military event for which the propertyless class were recruited. If the *proletarii* were recruited after the Pyrrhic War, we should expect information on this score in connection with the Second Punic War, since the sources for this war are relatively detailed and the manpower shortage encountered was so severe that the authorities decided to recruit criminals [83] and slaves [84] to the legions. If the *proletarii* were indeed recruited, it seems improbably that Livy and perhaps also Polybius, who described the war in detail, would not have

(77) Liv., XXII, 57.

(78) In P.-W., *R.-E.*, s.v. *dilectus*, col. 606, is indicated that the poor served in the navy as sailors — *nautae* and not as soldiers — *milites classici*.

(79) IV, 1, 3.

(80) *de Ciu. Dei*, III, 17.

(81) Peter, *H.R.R.*, I, p. 105, fr. 21.

(82) Gell., XVI, 10, 1.

(83) Liv., XXIII, 14.

(84) Liv., XXII, 57.

mentioned such a significant fact. This is especially true of Livy, who would hardly have referred to the recruitment of criminals and slaves without mentioning the mobilization of the *proletarii*. Moreover Augustinus too, in his description of the calamities and the hardships suffered by pagan Rome, mentioned that on the eve of the Pyrrhic War, due to a shortage of soldiers, the propertyless class were recruited, while during the Second Punic War slaves and criminals were drafted for the same reason ([85]). On the other hand, he does not state that the propertyless class were again recruited in this war. This silence can hardly be accidental. It is probable that, during the Second Punic War, the authorities were careful to observe the formal requirements of the law and did not actually recruit propertyless persons to the legions. At the same time, they used a legal device to turn part of the *capite censi* into *assidui*, in order to recruit some propertyless persons for the legions. In the year 214 B.C., the minimum property requirement for the *assidui* class was lowered from 11,000 to 4,000 asses ([86]) and the new *assidui* were legally eligible for service in the legions. Thus the law was maintained even during a time of extreme *tumultus maximus* and when there was a very severe shortage of soldiers.

However, Gellius reports that the poet Julius Paulus had said in the course of an informal conversation, that the *proletarii* were recruited during difficult times, when there was a shortage of young men. Paulus' words, as quoted by Gellius, were : ... *neque proletarii neque capite censi milites, nisi in tumultu maximo scribebantur* ([87]) and further on : *proletariorum tamen ordo honestior aliquanto et re et nomine quam capite censorum fuit nam et asperis reipublicae temporibus, cum iuuentutis inopia esset in militiam tumultuariam legebantur armaque in sumptu publico praebebantur* ([88]). This appears to constitute clear evidence that the propertyless class were recruited into the army, and therefore fell into the category of *Qui arma ferre possent*. But the reliability and value of this quotation should be carefully considered. It is immediately evident that these words were neither spoken by a historian nor were they taken from a scholarly work, whether historical or philological. They do not even refer back to a literary text. They are the words of a poet, uttered during

(85) *de Ciu. Dei*, III, 18.

(86) See E. GABBA, *op. cit.*, p. 181 ff. His argumentation is strong and convincing. BRUNT has the same opinion, *op. cit.*, pp. 66 and 403.

(87) *Noc. Att.*, XVI, 10, 11.

(88) *Noc. Att.*, XVI, 10, 12-13.

an informal conversation. Even though Gellius states that Julius Paulus was a very learned man, these words were said impromptu and, in mentioning the *proletarii*, Paulus neither relied on, nor even mentioned any sources (as he did in speaking about the *capite censi* being taken into the legions by Marius, when he cited Sallust as his proof, or in other matters which he mentioned in that same conversation, and for which he referred to the Twelve Tablets as his source). The words quoted above were said on the basis of an impression founded on general vaguely remembered knowledge, and can therefore hardly be relied on as proof of anything. Let us now examine his actual words. Paulus told his listeners, during that conversation, that there was a distinction between *proletarii* and *capite censi*. According to him, the *proletarii* were those whose property was below 1,500 *asses* but above 375. Those who owned less than 375 *asses* were the *capite censi*. This assertion accords neither with the statement made by Festus (89), identifying the *capite censi* with the *proletarii*, nor with that of Cicero (90), who used the term *proletarii* for all those whose property was less than 1,500 *asses*. Attempts have been made to resolve the contradiction between Gellius on the one hand, and Festus and Cicero on the other, but these have had no sound factual basis and have been acknowledged as being extremely hypothetical (91). Who was wrong, therefore — Paulus, or Festus and Cicero?

Paulus said that, in times of emergency, the *proletarii* served in the army but the *capite censi* did not. The latter were first drafted into the army by Marius (92). On the basis of this statement it might be assumed that, when conducting the census, the censors differentiated between the *capite censi* and the *proletarii* in their lists, or at least noted down to which category each person belonged. This may have been the case, but we have no evidence for it. Moreover, it is not very likely that this was so, for what purpose would have been achieved by making a precise record of the property of those who were not *assidui*? All the propertyless persons were included in one *centuria* in the *comitia centuriata*, and none of them either paid any taxes or served in the legions (in normal times). The question that remains, therefore, is whether the differentiation between categories or the exact registration of property was instituted only for the purpose of recruiting the *proletarii* into the legions in the rare case of an

(89) P. 226.
(90) *De Rep.*, II, 40.
(91) See Kübler, in P.W., *R.-E.*, s.v. *capite censi*, col. 1523.
(92) *Noc. Att.*, XVI, 10, 14.

emergency or a severe shortage of soldiers? Since it seems unlikely that the authorities would have been able to anticipate the need to recruit the *proletarii*, it is improbable that they exercised such extreme caution about registration, although this may have been the case. So much for logical considerations. Let us now examine the facts. E. Gabba has shown convincingly (93) that only after the year 133 B.C. were 1,500 *asses* taken as the minimum property requirement for inclusion in the category of *assidui*. Julius Paulus had stated, as already noted, that those whose property was less than 1,500 *asses* but more than 375 served in the army during times of emergency, but when were there such times of emergency after the year 133 B.C. and before the recruitment of the propertyless class into the legions by Marius? Paulus may have been mistaken only as regards the number of *asses* he mentioned, but no in his actual statement that the propertyless class were divided into the not so poor, who were mobilized, and the absolute paupers, who were never called upon to serve. His obvious mistake as to the number of *asses* makes us prefer Festus, who certainly checked his statements and made use of written sources, as well as Cicero, who was close to the period, to the chance conversation of a poet.

Furthermore, no historical event could have been more appropriately defined as *tumultus maximus* than the Second Punic War and never did Rome suffer more from a manpower shortage than at that time. Nevertheless, we have no scrap of information linking the data Gellius gives us with the recruitment methods used during the war with Hannibal. Moreover, if Paulus was right it is surprising that Polybius, who thought fit to mention that the propertyless class served in the navy (94) at a time when the navy was in a neglected condition, did not find it necessary to state that in times of emergency the not so poor members of the same class were recruited. The fact that Cicero, who was very well versed in the Roman constitution, attributed to Servius Tullius the stipulation that 1,500 *asses* were the minimum amount for inclusion in the class of *assidui* (95), shows that, even in the middle of the first century B.C., when the *De Republica* was being written, the information on this point was unreliable. It is not surprising, therefore, that Julius Paulus' words do not correspond to the facts in our possession, for they are based on an unchecked piece of information on a matter which was evidently

(93) *Op. cit.*, p. 184 ff.
(94) VI, 19.
(95) *L.c.*

transmitted in a distorted form in historical writings. We can only partly explain the origin of Paulus' mistakes. It is not really possible to find the source for the distinction between *proletarii* and *capite censi*, but we can find the source for the statement that the *proletarii* were recruited before Marius' time. Paulus, as has been stated above, asserted that during a time of emergency — *tumultus* — the *proletarii* were recruited. For this there is no evidence except during the Pyrrhic War. It may, however, be assumed that Paulus confused *tumultus* as a situation with *tumultus* meaning the recruitment method. Besides the usual draft, which was carried out in Rome on the basis of censors' registration lists, there was a rapid method of mass recruitment implemented by the consuls, called *tumultus*. By this method the consul would go to a certain area drafting anyone he found. In emergency recruitment of this kind, which was not carried out on the basis of censors' registration lists, no one bothered to find out the recruit's age, years of service or property. Thus, *proletarii alias capite censi* could be recruited. In this case they were *qui arma ferre possent*. During the census, by contrast, a list of those *ciues qui arma ferre possent*, who were drafted in the usual way, was made. In that recruitment their age, property, and length of time in service were taken into account. Regarding the recruitment of *proletarii*, it is not advisable to place inordinate reliability on a fragment of a sentence, *expedito pauperem plebeium atque proletarium*, which has remained from a speech by Cato (96), for we do not know to what he was referring and in which context it was said.

As stated above, Polybius formulated the significance of the total of Roman and Italian manpower as follows : τῶν δυναμένων ὅπλα βαστάξειν. For our purposes it is important to examine this statement in regard to Roman manpower. When he said that τῶν δυναμένων ὅπλα βαστάξειν enumerated a certain number, did this figure include the *capite censi* or only the *assidui*, who were, from the point of view of the census, *qui arma ferre possent*? This examination is significant with regard to the census figure, because the figures Polybius mentions in relation to the extent of Roman manpower were probably based on this number (97). Therefore, the interpretation of Polybius' figures is a key to understanding the census figure.

Our point of departure in resolving this problem will be the terms used by Polybius : πεζοί and ἱππεῖς. He was well aware of the fact that the

(96) *O.R.F.*², 58, n. 152.
(97) Brunt, *op. cit.*, p. 46.

capite censi were not πεζοί. While it is, therefore, most probable that the numbers he mentions include only the *assidui*, a careless use of the term cannot be disregarded. But was Polybius careless? He tells us that in the year 225 B.C. the Roman infantry numbered 49,200 Romans and Campanians and the cavalry 3,100 Romans and Campanians. Besides these figures of soldiers who were in active service he mentions two other figures, — 250,000 Roman and Campanian infantry, 23,000 Roman and Campanian cavalry (98). He adduces these two numbers as the manpower figures recorded in the registers. For our purposes, as will be clarified below, it is very important to establish whether the last two figures included the former two or whether all Roman manpower was the sum of the four figures, i.e. the sum of soldiers under arms and the men listed in the registers. It is quite clear that Polybius thought that the total manpower was the sum of the four figures, namely 325,300. This can be learned from the simple fact that the total figure of Italian and Roman manpower cited by him is the sum of the numbers he mentions, namely, the number of soldiers in active service and the number of men in the registration lists (99). However, important modern historians maintain that Polybius was mistaken and that the number he gives according to the lists also included infantry and cavalry in active service (100). In other words, the total of Roman manpower was only 273.000. The question which remains is whether Polybius was mistaken or not. Orosius provides important information for refuting the argument that Polybius was in error, by stating that the Roman forces at that time numbered 348,000 infantry and 26,600 cavalry (101). Although the figure for the infantry differs from the one Polybius mentions, the larger number leaves room for the assumption that the total amount of Roman infantry comprised both active servicemen and those who were registered. Mommsen, who accepted Polybius' numerical data at face value (102), assumed that a mistake had been made in Orosius' manuscript and adjusted the number

(98) II, 24.

(99) See also BELOCH, *Bevölkerung*, p. 361 ; AFZELIUS, *Eroberung*, p. 98 ; TOYNBEE, *op. cit.*, p. 482 ; BRUNT, *op. cit.*, pp. 44-45.

(100) F. W. WALBANK, *A Historical Commentary on Polybius*, Oxford, 1957, p. 198 ; TOYNBEE, *op. cit.*, pp. 482-483 ; BRUNT, *op. cit.*, p. 45 ff. ; and also in *C.A.H.*, VIII, p. 811. We do not know anything about those lists. Any statement that they were the census figure is therefore hypothetical and without a real basis. The conclusion that they comprised the active soldiers has to be proved.

(101) IV, 13, 6.

(102) *Röm. Forsch.*, II, pp. 386-387 ; also LIEBENAM, in P.W., *R.-E.*, s.v. *dilectus*, col. 608.

of infantry from 348,200 to 298,200 ([103]). His correction was based on altering the figure C in the total to L. Niebuhr, on the other hand, suggested correcting the number by deleting the C and putting the number at only 248,200 ([104]). The total force according to Mommsen numbered about 325,000 and according to Niebuhr about 270,000. Niebuhr's correction was of course accepted by those scholars who thought Polybius has been wrong ([105]).

In deciding whether to accept Mommsen's or Niebuhr's opinion, an examination of the numbers themselves can prejudice us toward one side or the other but does not give a conclusive answer. The resemblance between the two figures C and L makes a confusion between them in the manuscript a reasonable probability. However, it is also possible that a C was added inadvertently ([106]). One should, therefore, be careful about drawing any clear-cut conclusions from a comparison of the numbers of infantry given by Orosius and Polybius. On the other hand, it must also be stressed that it seems easier to mistake L for C as a result of carelessness than to omit a figure. For this reason the first possibility is to be preferred over the second. However, it is not necessary to make such a choice, for the number of cavalry mentioned by Orosius is, to my mind, decisive. The number is *XXVI milia sescenti*, i.e. 26,600 cavalry. The correction to 23,100 which is sometimes made is arbitrary and forced and is not justified by the number itself. It seems improbable that such a strange mistake was made in *sescenti*, whereas the supposition that the number was XXIII is groundless and is based solely on the assumption that the total number of cavalry in Polybius' manpower list is identical with their number on the register rather than being the outcome of adding the number of men registerered to the number of active soldiers. This constitutes a clear case of altering facts to fit a theory. The figures for cavalry given by Polybius are 3,100 in active service and 23,000 registered. Orosius' figure is, therefore, close to the sum of these two numbers. Thus, if there is no doubt that the total figure was the sum of the two numbers, namely, those registered and those serving, there is no reason to suppose that this was not also the case with regard to the infantry, all the more so because, as stated above, Mommsen's correction

(103) *Op. cit.*, p. 388 ff.

(104) *R.G.*, II², 81.

(105) BELOCH, *Bevölkerung*, p. 363 ; BRUNT, *op. cit.*, p. 46.

(106) The number is CCCXXXXVIIICC. In Teubner's edition the correction CC*L*XXXXVIIICC appears.

is more acceptable than Niebuhr's. The total of Roman and Campanian forces in 225 B.C. was therefore 325,000. This may also be proved in another way. The census figure for the year 234/3, the last one preserved from before the Second Punic War, was 270,713 ([107]), whereas the census figure for 204/3 was 214,000 ([108]). If the total manpower figure for the year 225 was not greater than the census figure for 234/3 being only 270,000 Romans and Campanians, this would mean that the figure for the census immediately prior to the Second Punic War was also approximately 270,000 or slightly more. This view, which is held by Beloch, Toynbee, Brunt and others, indicates that the 204/3 census figure was reduced by about 55,000, despite the fact that the figure Polybius mentions explicitly includes the Campanians (and it is clear that they were not included in the census figure for this year) ([109]) and despited the heavy casualities suffered by the Romans during the Second Punic War. It seems hardly probable that the decline was so slight. Roman losses during the Second Punic War up to the year 204 were as follows ([110]) : in the battle on the river Trebia, Roman losses were few. At the Trasimene Lake almost two legions were wiped out, namely, approximately 10,000 Romans. In the Cannae battle, according to Livy, 54,700 men were killed or captured. Appian gives the number of dead as 55,000 as well as a large number taken captive. Polybius gives the number of dead and captured as being 85,630. There are grounds for assuming that Polybius exaggerated. Consequently, probably approximately 60,000 men died or were captured, meaning that the Roman army lost about 30,000 Roman citizens. At the end of 216 two Roman legions were wiped out at Silva Litana on the land of the Boii. In 212, two legions were slaughtered at *ager Beneuentanus* and two more at Herdonia. In 211 the greater part of the Roman army was destroyed in Spain, and in 210 two legions were crushed at Herdonia. Besides the loss of entire legions the Romans also suffered smaller blows. In 218 1,200 Romans were killed in the land of the Boii and in 217, following the Battle of Trasimene, 4,000 Romans were killed or captured. In 212, 7,000 men were killed, half of them Romans. In 209, 5,700 men from Marcellus' army were killed in North-

(107) Liv., *Per.* XX.

(108) Liv., XXIX, 37.

(109) Capua in 211 was deprived of her corporate personality. Surely her citizens were deprived of their Roman citizenship. Beloch's opinion that they remained *ciues sine suffragio* is improbable. See his book *Campanien*, Roma, 1964, p. 320.

(110) See Toynbee's casualties description in *Hannibal's Legacy*, II, p. 15 ff.

West Apulia. In 208 a Roman force numbering 3,500 men, was crushed near Petelia, 2,000 being killed and 1,500 captured. It may be said with certainty that up till the year 204 at least 90,000 Roman citizens were killed. Apart from military losses, the Roman population suffered from a plague which broke out in 208 (111). Livy does not stipulate how many people died as a result. If we assume that the figure cited by Polybius, i.e. 270,000, was the census figure and that this increased to 280,000 or slightly more just before the Second Punic War, and we subtract from it the number of Campanians — approximately 20-30,000 — and the number of death from the pestilence, we would obtain a total close to 160,000, which is lower by 55,000 than the census figure for the year 204/3 B.C. On the other hand, if we subtract the total number of losses plus the Capuan manpower estimate added to the dead from pestilence, from the figure 325,000, which is the total of all those recorded in the registers together with active servicemen, the figure obtained would be close to that of the 204/3 census. Simple arithmetic shows that the figure reached is around 205,000, but the element of natural increase should be taken into account. Thus, since the numerical data at our disposal is inaccurate and there are no figures regarding natural increase and the victims of pestilence, the figure of 325,000 accords with that of 214,000. At any rate it is closer than the number 270,000 or 280,000. Toynbee's attempt — in a different context — to use natural increase alone to explain the slight decline of 55,000 in the census figure for the year 204/3 (112) lacks any real validity. His argument that the natural increase was 67,000 between the years 179/8 and 164/3 and the same was also during the war years is misguided and hardly merits discussion. Clearly the growth of 67,000 was not the outcome of natural increase alone, for this would mean an average natural increase of about 2% per year, which seems highly unlikely for Roman society at that time. Moreover, within the five years between 174/3 and 169/8 the population grew by 43,000, implying a natural increase of more than 3% per year, a rate which not even Egypt and India have attained today. It is clear, therefore, that the high growth rate could not have been the outcome of natural increase alone. Other things have to be taken into account, such as the manumission of slaves, the conferring of full citizenship on the *municipia* and possible negligence in census registration resulting in the inclusion of Latins residing in Rome

(111) Liv., XXVII, 23, 6-7.
(112) *Op. cit.*, I, p. 476 ff.

after the year 173 or thronged to the city after that date. Thus, from all the above, it can be stated quite conclusively that Polybius was not in error and that the total Roman manpower figure for the year 225 B.C. was the sum of active soldiers and those listed on the registers.

The interpretation of the growth in manpower from 270,713 Roman citizens in the 234/3 census to 325,000 Roman and Campanian citizens in 225, as derived from Polybius, contributes to clarifying the issue of whether the *capite censi* were included in the census figure. No doubt Polybius' numbers were based on data from the census held after that of 234/3. The numerical rise in Polybius' figures is the outcome of two factors, the inclusion of the Campanians, who were not, in my opinion, included in the census figure, and the increase in the census figure used by Polybius. The first factor can be estimated, for in the year 216 there were 34,000 Campanian *iuniores* [(113)]. It can be assumed therefore, that Polybius' figures included between 25,000 and 30,000 Campanians. The fact that there may have been inaccurate reporting of Campanians before 225 B.C. should also be taken into account. The greater accuracy in later reporting may have been the result of Rome's special concern prior to the outbreak of the Second Punic War or shortly afterwards. If this is so the figure the Campanians reported was lower than those I have given.

Be that as it may, it can be established that the census figure on which Polybius based his date was larger by at least 25-30,000 than that of the previous census. This rise cannot derive from natural increase, since it is much greater than the growth trend in the figures of the preceding censuses. An average natural increase rate of 2%, given the sanitary conditions of the time, hardly seems possible. In accounting for this it should be noted that in 232 B.C. land was distributed among Roman citizens in the *ager Gallicus et Picenus*. Following this settlement movement, which took place after the 234/3 census and before the census used by Polybius, it can be assumed that many *capite censi* became *assidui*. This could have been because of the land distribution itself, if it was considered *ager priuatus*, or because of the value of the produce, if it was considered *ager publicus*. It may well have been therefore, that this increase was a result of Flaminius' activity. Following the change in their status the *capite censi* who had become *assidui* were included in the census figure, which had not previously been the case. It may be estimated that they caused a rise of between 10-20,000 in the census

(113) Liv., XXIII, 5, 15.

figure. This explanation reinforces the probability that Polybius used the term πεζοί carefully. Thus, when speaking of τῶν δυναμένων ὅπλα βαστάζειν he probably meant only *assidui*, since the *capite censi* were not πεζοί. Since Polybius' figures were based on the census prior to 225, it can be concluded that this figure did not comprise *capite censi*.

The only conspicuous rise in the census figure following the first census held after the Second Punic War and before Tiberius Gracchus' tribuneship is that recorded in the census of 169/8 B.C. That figure rose by 43,790. During this period land was recorded as being distributed to Roman citizens by *assignatio uiritim* only once, in 173 B.C. Can it have been mere chance that the only rise followed the sole land-distribution of this kind recorded? Or did those *capite censi* who received the land upon becoming *assidui* contribute to the increase?

A clear example of the connection between the increase in the census figure and the distribution of land among Roman citizens can be seen in the figure for 125 B.C. which amounted to 394,736 *capita ciuium* ([114]), representing a rise of 75,913 citizens as compared with the census figure for 131/0. Many scholars of note, believing that the figure includes the *capite censi*, have tried to disregard the connection between the numerical increase and the distribution of land, interpreting the increase in a variety of strange ways. They did not accept the most obvious and natural explanation, namely that the *capite censi* who received land became *assidui* and, following the change in their status, were included in the census figure, causing the increase.

I will first review the various interpretations, attempting to evaluate them, after which I will show why the distribution of land should be considered to be the immediate cause of the rise in the census figure for 125 B.C.

Beloch, maintained that the number of 394,736 was the outcome of a mistake made in the manuscript, possibly by a copyist ([115]). He maintained that the figure C had been added to the beginning of the number, which had originally been 294,736. This interpretation is both groundless and unacceptable, since it suggests a decline of 24,087 in comparison with the previous census, held in 131/0 B.C. A decline as drastic as this, which would have been the worst in the entire second century B.C., is completely improbable since it would have occurred precisely at the point when there was an improvement in the situation of some of the poor —

(114) Liv., *Per.* LX.
(115) *Bevölkerung*, p. 312.

through the distribution of land — and when part of the census evaders would have benefitted from appearing before the censors in 125. The sharpest drop in the census figure to occur in the second century, was in the year 136/5, the last census held before Tiberius Gracchus' tribuneship. The decline was 9,509 in comparison with the preceding census, at a time when the social crisis was at its most acute. It seems unlikely therefore, that after the tribuneship of Tiberius Gracchus there would have been a decline two-and-a-half-times as great, for the downward trend had been checked as my be inferred from the 131/0 B.C. census. The figure of the latter census had risen by a few hundred in comparison with the preceding one. Consequently, the correction suggested by Beloch should be rejected altogether.

Lange (116) has connected the rise in the census figure with the awarding of citizenship to the allies after the destruction of Fregellae. However, not only is there no mention of this in the sources, it is also improbable in the light of the Senate's firm policy towards that colony and its opposition to Gaius Gracchus' suggestions that citizenship be awarded to the allies (117).

Carcopino argues (118) that the numerical rise stems from the manumission of slaves by the aristocracy, who tried in this way to consolidate their influence in the popular assembly. This is not mentioned in the sources and, moreover, the active assembly at that time was the one organized by the tribes and not the *comitia centuriata* ; therefore, since the *libertini* voted only in the four urban tribes, it seems improbable that the aristocracy undertook large-scale manumission in order to exert very little influence. Similarly, there is no basis in the sources for Carcopino's opinion, almost identical to Lange's, that the Latins were granted citizenship. The claims used to refute Lange's argument are equally applicable here. T. Frank maintains (119) that the censors did not take care to register the *capite censi* in the census figure, in spite of the fact that they were included, because of their lack of importance. However, when they became military potential, as a result of the land distribution, there was good cause for registering them carefully and therefore the 125 census figure is higher. In addition, the *proletarii* themselves wanted to be

(116) *Römische Altertümer*, III², p. 27.

(117) Rejection of this theory see BELOCH, *Bevölkerung*, p. 351.

(118) *Histoire romaine*, II², p. 234.

(119) *Economic Survey*, I, p. 329. His opinion is accepted by BRUNT, *op. cit.*, p. 77 ff. and by H. LAST, *C.A.H.*, IX, p. 43.

registered in order to be eligible for land distribution benefits. This interpretation does not ring true for a number of reasons. First, this concerns a rise of about 20% in the total number of persons registered. If this rise was the result of greater accuracy, we could assume that in 125/4 there were still many *proletarii* who had not been registered. Therefore, the inaccuracy in previous censuses might have constituted more than 20%. Although this hypothesis may be correct, there is no evidence whatsoever that negligence on this scale existed. Secondly, whereas even before the rise of Tiberius Gracchus the Senate tended to ease the burden of recruitment on the citizens (as reflected by the law of 140 B.C., which forbade more than one recruitment being held in any one year) ([120]), after his tribuneship it transferred the brunt of the burden of army service from the citizens to the allies. This policy was reflected by the fact that before 133 the ratio of soldiers from among the citizens to those from among the allies had been 1 : 1 ([121]), while after this date it changed to 1 : 2 ([122]), so that the burden placed on the allies was twice as heavy as that of the citizens. There is, therefore, no basis for arguing that the Senate wished to solve the recruitment problem by increasing Roman manpower potential for service in the legions and consequently gave instructions that land-recipients should be registered accurately. Thirdly, if the *capite censi* who were not enumerated in the census really wanted to be registered in order to enjoy the benefits of the reform, why did they not present themselves to the censors in 131/0 B.C. when the Commission of Three was at the height of its activity, rather than doing so only in 125/4 B.C. when the Commission's activity was on the wane because it was restricted by the intervention of Scipio Aemilianus in 129? It seems improbable that the *proletarii* would want to be registered at a time when the distribution of land was slackening rather than when it was at its peak and, presumably, the ensuing publicity was at its height.

There is no confirmation in any of the sources for Brunt's assumption, intended to support T. Frank's suggestion, that the land distribution began a few years after the Commission's activity ([123]), and certainly after the 131/0 B.C. census. This supposedly explains why the increase in the census figure does not occur in that year but only in the census of 125/4 B.C., when the land recipients were registered. However, there are signs

(120) Liv., *Per.* LIV.
(121) Brunt, *op. cit.*, p. 681 ff.
(122) Brunt, *op. cit.*, p. 685 ff.
(123) *Op. cit.*, p. 79 ff.

that the distribution of land began shortly after Tiberius' assassination. The Senate agreed to the land reform not because of its importance but in order to appease the masses, who were in a turmoil after the murders and mass-imprisonments [124]. The Senate would naturally have given priority to land-distribution in order to appease the population. The famous inscription *C.I.L.*, I, 628 can be adduced as proof of this if it was written by the Consul Pupilias Laenas [125], who held this office in 132 B.C., soon after Tiberius' assassination. The author of the inscription boasted that he was the first to have forced pasture-owners to vacate their lands for the benefit of farmers. If Pupilias Laenas was indeed the author, as I believe, we are dealing here with someone who, though outspokenly anti-Gracchan and not a member of the Commission of Three, nevertheless acted in accordance with the Gracchan reform. This can be explained by the fact that it was in the Senate's interest to implement the reform and indicates that land was distributed immediately after Tiberius' tribuneship and before the 131/0 census. As the Senate desired to pacify the mob, it may also have distributed land through the offices of others of its representatives at that time, and instructed the Commission of Three to accelerate the distribution. If the Commission dealt mainly with legal affairs in the early years of its activity, trying to define and measure public lands and private property, as Brunt thinks, it is hard to understand the masses' hostility towards Scipio Aemilianus in 129 for transferring jurisdiction regarding definitions of land status from the Commissions of Three to the Consul [126].

If the situation was as Brunt assumed, judicial matters were not of great moment for the masses in 129 B.C., for large stretches of land which had already been defined as *ager publicus* had not yet been distributed and there was no reason to fear that land would not be distributed to them. Moreover, from Appian's description it can be learned that legal action and land distribution went hand in hand. Appian writes that the crowd's anger was directed at Scipio Aemilianus not when he brought his motion before the Senate, but only after the Consul Tuditanus had left the judiciary, whereupon the Commission stopped functioning [127] and no

(124) Plut., *Tib.*, 21.

(125) So Mommsen, *C.I.L.*, I, 2, pp. 509-510. Rejection of this opinion, see T. D. Wiseman, *Viae Anniae*, in *P.B.S.R.*, XXXII (1964), p. 21 ff. ; P. Fraccaro, *op. cit.*, pp. 55-56 ; Astin, *op. cit.*, pp. 353-354. In my opinion the arguments for the refutation are interesting but not convincing. They do not refute Mommsen's arguments.

(126) App., *B.C.*, I, 19.

(127) *B.C.*, I, 19.

land was distributed. Appian may have erred in saying that the Commission ceased to function, but the distribution of land may have slowed down, at least temporarily, during that year. The populace was angry because it had received hardly any land and was therefore open to incitement based on the claim that the agrarian law was about to be abrogated. Appian linked the halt in land distribution with the cessation of legal activity, stating that the Commission of Three stopped functioning soon after Tuditanus left Rome. This would imply that legal activity and the distribution of land were implemented in close connection with one another. It seems clear, therefore, that Brunt's assumption is unacceptable.

Beloch denied that the rise in the census figure of 125 B.C. had been caused by the land distribution implemented by the Commission of Three, since he thought it had stopped functioning in 129, leaving insufficient time to distribute large tracts of land, and certainly not to approximately 75,000 people. Consequently, only a few *capite censi* became *assidui* as a result of the reform, amounting to far less than the increase in the 125 B.C. census figure. This argument may be countered by pointing out that there is no information about the scope of the Commission's activity up to 129 B.C. and it may have distributed considerable amounts of land in the four years of its full activity. Furthermore, there is no proof that the reform measures were stopped, on the contrary there are grounds for believing that they continued. Appian, on whom Beloch relied, relates that after Scipio Aemilianus intervened, the legal authority to define *ager publicus* and *ager priuatus* was taken away from the Commission, but this does not mean that the Commission's activities stopped altogether. Appian states that it was paralyzed because Tuditanus, who was consul and should have accepted legal authority, preferred to abandon his task and leave for Illyria. There is no proof, however, that the consuls of the following years also neglected their duties.

Livy ([128]) asserts that after Scipio Aemilianus' death the Commission continued to sow dissension, indicating that it had not ceased to function. Dio states ([129]) that after Scipio's death the Commission continued its activities throughout Italy and, in his words, ruined all of it. There is room for doubting his testimony for he drew his information from a tradition very hostile to Tiberius Gracchus, but it constitutes evidence of the continued activity of the Commission on a large scale. A basis for the

(128) Liv., *Per.* 59.
(129) Frag. 84, 2.

conjecture that the Commission managed to distribute a considerable amount of land may be found in the fact that Gaius Gracchus went to North-Africa in order to found a colony there (130). He may have been forced to go there because of the scarcity of land in Italy. Another possibility is that after 129 the Commission was left with large tracts of land defined as *ager publicus*, whose legal status was beyond doubt. This was especially true for much territory in southern Italy, which had been expropriated from the allies after the Second Punic War because they had joined Hannibal's side. The large scale of confiscation implies that the status of much of the land was clearly *ager publicus*. Beloch's argument is, therefore, far from convincing. The land may have been distributed to fewer than 75,000 people, thus failing to account for the total rise in the census figure, but Gabba has shown that there is also a connection between the increase and the lowering of the minimum property requirement for consideration as an *assiduus* from 4,000 to 1,500 (131). His contention that this probably occurred between 133 and 123 B.C. seems convincing. Thus, the new *assidui* contributed to the rise in the census figure. He interprets the rise as stemming entirely from the fact that the *capite censi* became *assidui*, partly through the lowering of the minimum property requirement and partly through the distribution of land. His opinion is that the *capite censi* were not included in the census figure. Evidence that the census figure rose as a result of the land-distribution may be inferred from the fact that it rose significantly not in the first census after the land reform, but in the second one, in 125 B.C. From the *Lex Agraria* of the year 111 B.C. (132) it transpires that the land distributed as a result of the land reform was not taken into account by the censors as part of an assessee's property. Thus the awarding of land to the *capite censi* did not change their status and did not turn them into *assidui*. This makes it clear why the 131/0 census figure rose by only 890 in comparison with that of 136/5. On the other hand, after a number of years farmers had had an opportunity to acquire some property and save enough money to attain the required minimum, which was exceedingly low, and become *assidui*. Assessable property consisted of agricultural implements, slaves, clothes, jewellery, cash money, loans and anything else belonged to the assessee (133) (land, as stated above, was not assessed

(130) E. G. Hardy, *Six Roman Laws*, p. 39 ; *C.A.H.*, IX, p. 44 ; Earl, *op. cit.*, p. 26.
(131) *Op. cit.*, pp. 184-187.
(132) L. 8.
(133) Th. Mommsen, *St. R.*, II, p. 369, n. 4 ; Brunt, *op. cit.*, p. 15.

in this case). Since the buying power of 1,500 asses was very low [134], the value of the buildings, agricultural implements and money saved by the farmer would exceed this minimum after a certain time. This fact was reflected in the census of the year 125/4 though not in the one of 131/0.

In sum, I think I have been able to show that it is possible to refute the arguments of those scholars who have attempted to prove that the *capite censi* were included in the census figures. No convincing arguments have been presented to justify the thesis that there is no direct connection between the distribution of land and the rise in the census figure. This link has been indicated by me on the only three occasions when land distribution was implemented, and the census figures following closely after them may be accepted as authentic, namely, that of 232 B.C., that of 173 B.C. and the one carried out by the Gracchan Commission. Furthermore, I have demonstrated that from the point of view of census registration the *capite censi* were not considered *Qui arma ferre possent*, and since this was the category of citizens included in the census figure, this constitutes additional proof of the fact that the *capite censi* were not included in the census figure.

Undoubtedly, the question under discussion is an inseparable part of a much larger complex of problems concerning the condition of Roman society, its administration and manpower at the time. There are many imponderables which make it difficult to probe the question of Roman manpower, and any attempt to solve them must be based on tentative assumptions. However, the one irrefutable fact is that the census figures at the time of the republic were in the hundreds of thousands while in Augustus' time they reached millions. The minimalistic thesis proposed by Beloch and accepted by Brunt which maintains that the great numerical leap can be explained by a change in the principles guiding the census, namely, that Augustus also included women and children in the figures, has no direct basis in the sources. Brunt's monumental and brilliant attempt to show that the number of male Roman citizens in Augustus' period was only about one-and-a-half million encountered many difficulties which cannot be discussed here. Let it suffice here to point out that in order to prove his thesis, Brunt was forced to estimate the male population in Cisalpine Gaul as being 300,000. However, in this district there were about 80 colonies, *municipia* and many villages. Some of the cities such as Placentia, Cremona, Aquileia, Mediolanum,

(134) See next chapter, p. 67-8.

Patavium, Ariminum, Verona, Ravenna and others were large. His numerical estimate is therefore questionable. The figure for the population of Cisalpine Gaul alone raises doubts concerning the estimate of all male Roman citizens in the Empire at the time. On the other hand, my assumption that the *capite censi* were not included in the census figure does contribute to explaining the immense increase in the census figures during Augustus' time.

After the military reform introduced by Marius, the status of *capite censi* lost its significance as a separate class. It is possible that the status was also legally abrogated and did not exist at all at the end of the Republic. This may have been the case when the *Tabula Heracleana* was written. This *Tabula* contains the statement that when a census was held in Rome, the officials of the different cities had to enumerate their citizens ([135]), namely including the poor. In Augustus' census, therefore, the poor, who were considered *capite censi* during the Republic, were included. In the year 70 B.C., when the status of *capite censi* evidently still existed legally, this class was not included in the census figure, which stood at 910,000 *capite ciuium*. The registration of the propertyless, who no longer constituted a separate class, and their inclusion in the census figure by Augustus can partially explain the large discrepancy between the numbers. Equally, the considerable discrepancy between the census figure from the end of the Republic and that from Augustus' time gives grounds for assuming that the *capite censi* were not included in the census figure.

Nevertheless, although they were not included in these figures, this does not mean that they did not report to the censors and were not registered in any way. Clearly, it was important, that their numbers should be ascertained even if they may only have served as sailors in the navy. It was also necessary to enumerate them for division into tribes. Their very name, *capite censi*, testifies to the fact that they were enumerated. There may well have been a separate list for them which was not included in the main register. Brunt attempted to refute such a possibility by claiming that if such a list had existed we should have known about it, just as we know about other separate lists kept to register different categories of people. This is unacceptable since it is well-known that our information concerning the census bureaucracy is meagre and

(135) *F.I.R.A.*, I, no. 13,145. It is difficult to know when the *Tabula* was written. The opinion is that it was written in Caesar's time, but there are doubts about that. There are no real proofs that the paragraph which deals with the census was written before 70 B.C.

fortuitous. It is, therefore, possible that there were separate lists of which we have no knowledge. Brunt himself presumed that other registration lists, like the *Tabulae Caeritum* for the citizens of Caere, existed for the other *municipia* which had the status of *sine suffragio*. Furthermore, the authorities had no special political, economic or military interest in ascertaining the number of *capite censi*, but after the First Punic War it was necessary to enumerate them for the purposes of naval service and, as said above, it was necessary to register them for tribal division. It seems very probable, consequently, that for these specific reasons there was a separate list for them just as there was for widows and orphans who were not included in the census figures either. In conclusion, the census figure should not be taken as evidence that on the eve of Tiberius Gracchus' appearance on the political scene the number of *assidui* was small and that the authorities' recruitment difficulties and resultant concern were the outcome of a sharp demographic decline in the class of people possessing the financial minimum required for army service.

II

The Problem of Recruitment for the Legions

a) The Arguments Used in Recent Studies

In his book, *Hannibal's Legacy*, A. J. Toynbee claims that the difficulties in raising troops for the Roman army during the second century B.C. were symptomatic of a serious demographic and social disease (1). Prior to Tiberius' appearance on the political scene the potential of Roman power had greatly diminished and Toynbee states: "The first Roman statesman who faced this critical demographic fact and introduced legislation with a view to dealing with it was Tiberius Gracchus" (2).

P. A. Brunt also maintains that the problem with which Tiberius Gracchus was confronted was that of difficulties in recruitment, and that this was due to the decline in the number of *assidui* caused by the dispossession of the small farmers from their land. It did not occur to Tiberius to recruit soldiers for the legions from the proletariat since his objective was to revive the class of small farmers (3). Both these important historians present the approach generally accepted in modern historical works (4), but the question is whether the problem of the difficulties in recruitment prior to Tiberius Gracchus' tribuneship has been adequately understood. An even more important point is whether Tiberius Gracchus' attitude to this issue has been properly understood. Modern scholarship has regarded the reasons for the recruitment difficulties from a different angle. In his interesting book, *Scipio Aemilianus*, Astin has emphasized

(1) *Hannibal's Legacy*, II, Oxford, 1965, p. 92.

(2) *Op. cit.*, p. 96.

(3) *Italian Manpower 225 B.C. - 14 A.D.*, Oxford, 1971, p. 75.

(4) For example K. B. Marsh, *A History of the Roman World from 146 to 30 B.C.*, London, 1953, p. 32; D. C. Earl, *Tiberius Gracchus*, Brussels, 1963 (*Collection Latomus*, LXVI), p. 26; H. Scullard, *From the Gracchi to Nero*, London, 1970, p. 22.

the unwillingness of the Roman citizens to be mobilised. He analyzed in depth the factors accounting for the Roman citizens' reluctance to join the legions, but at the same time considers the demographic element to have influenced the problem of recruitment (5), and he states explicitly that Tiberius Gracchus wanted to increase the number of Roman citizens who were eligible for recruitment, in order to overcome these difficulties (6). This statement does not differ from the accepted view.

Undoubtedly, an examination of the problems of recruitment on the eve of Tiberius Gracchus' tribuneship will help us to reach a better understanding of his solutions to the ills of the time. I shall attempt to show that no demographic problem existed, since the number of *assidui* exceeded by far that of the men who served in the Roman legions.

The basis for the assumption that the recruitment difficulties were demographic, deriving from the limited number of *assidui* (7), was unquestionably created by the background accounts of Tiberius Gracchus' tribuneship given by Appian (8) and Plutarch (9). Both authors emphasize the fact that the number of inhabitants in Italy had declined, but insufficient attention has been paid to the fact that Appian refers solely to the allies and not to Roman citizens (this has been discussed in greater detail in Chapter I), while Plutarch writes : *Τὴν 'Ιταλίαν ἅπασαν ὀλιγανδρίας ἐλευθέρων αἰσθέσθαι*, also stressing Italy as a whole and not solely the body of Roman citizens. Since it can be assumed, as I have pointed out elsewhere, that both Appian and Plutarch used a common source which emphasized the demographic-military problem with regard to the allies (10), this would indicate the Plutarch's description is based on this source and originally referred to the allies. Even were this not the case, I have already shown that he was influenced by a source which emphasized the pan-Italic aspect from a demographic-military viewpoint (11). Moreover, in his description of Tiberius Gracchus' tribuneship, Plutarch presents the citizens as the sole object of the reform, making no mention whatsoever of the demographic problem. This omission seems to derive from the fact that the sources he used did not connect this problem with

(5) Astin, *Scipio Aemilianus*, Oxford, 1967, p. 167 ff.

(6) *Op. cit.*, p. 196.

(7) The arguments are summarized in Astin, *op. cit.*, pp. 171-172.

(8) *B.C.*, 1, 7.

(9) *Tiberius Gracchus*, 8.

(10) See my article : *The Lex Agraria of 133 B.C. and the Italian Allies*, in *Athenaeum*, N.S. XLVIII, p. 34 ff.

(11) *Op. cit.*, p. 36.

the Roman citizens. If, on the other hand, his intention was to refer to the Roman citizens, his statement that Italy was devoid of freemen cannot be taken seriously, since the number of Roman citizens enumerated in the census was more than 300,000, while the number in the census of 70 B.C. was almost one million freemen ([12]). The question naturally arises whether it was only the numbers of allies which were depleted when the process of dispossession and emigration to the city of Rome also affected Roman citizens. This is clearly unacceptable. It is, however, doubtful whether both these sources reflect the actual situation, i.e. whether there was in effect a decline in the total number of allies.

Both items of information concerning the number of allies — namely, the outcome of the census held in 225 B.C. ([13]) and the muster of 70 B.C. — indicate that there was no reduction in their number. In the census of 225 B.C., 450,000 allies were enumerated, while by the muster of 70 B.C. by 500,000 new citizens, who had been allies before the war of the Marsi entered the list. Despite the fact that these figures are only partial and do not give the whole picture, they provide sufficient evidence to indicate that there was no reduction in the total number of allies. Apparently the sources employed by both Appian and Plutarch had been influenced by the propaganda claims made by the allies to the Roman Senate, only some of which were justified. The claims concerning the decrease in the population and the inability to send men to the army, which had been voiced during the Second Punic War and in 177 B.C., are well known. (This will be discussed at greater length in the section of the next chapter dealing with recruitment among allies.) If assertions of this type were made by the allies in 177 B.C., it is evident that they increased in the years which followed, when there was a growing tendency for the population to move to urban centres. Not a few settlements which suffered from a population decline most probably claimed that they were unable to provide the quota of soldiers imposed upon them. It is highly likely that other settlements took advantage of the general atmosphere and made similar claims unjustifiably, as was done by the twelve colonies at the time of the Second Punic War. Be that as it may, the impression was created that the numbers of the allies had diminished. This may have been correct with regard to a certain number of areas, but the overall numbers of the allies did not decline, since other places flourished and the number of their

(12) Livius, *Epit.* XCVIII, Phelgon, F.12.6 (Jacoby, no. 257). 910,000 men according to Phelgon and 900,000 according to Livy.

(13) Polyb., II, 24.

inhabitants, as a result of the population shift, increased. Thus, not only do neither Appian nor Plutarch refer to the body of Roman citizens, but their assertions are also basically incorrect.

The census figure has also constituted a basis for the opinion that there was a sharp demographic decline in the mass of Roman citizens, but this is not proved by it. The figure itself indicates a continual increase throughout the first half of the second century B.C., from 243,703 men in the year 194/3 (14) (143,704 in Livy's text, but this appears to be an error) to 337,022 in 164/3 (15). This trend was, it is true, followed by a decline, but at its greatest this decline accounted for only 19,089 men, while the census of 136/5 gave the figure of 317,933 men (16). The drop was less than 6% and it was obviously far from constituting a crisis for Roman manpower. In this connection the question naturally arises whether these figures included the *capite censi*. In the previous chapter, I showed that there is a valid basis for assuming that they were not included ; but even if the reverse is true their numbers were not large, while, as I will demonstrate below, there are grounds for believing that the *assidui* were numerous.

The two reductions of the property minimum are also considered to provide evidence of the dearth of *assidui*, but the first one, from 11,000 to 4,000 *asses*, is irrelevant since it was implemented during the Second Punic War in 214 B.C. (17), while the second does not necessarily indicate a scarcity of *assidui*. It may well have been a result of the disinclination of the Roman citizens to be recruited. E. Gabba's convincing thesis that the reduction was undertaken after 133 B.C. and before 123 B.C. has already been cited in the previous chapter (18). His opinion, which I hold to be correct, is that the reduction contributed to the increase in the census figure for 125 B.C., i.e. that it was implemented before that year. It can easily be supposed that in the wake of the Senate's policy (which will be discussed below) of refraining from imposing the recruitment immoderately on the Roman citizens, it was decided to enlarge the ranks from which the men were to be drawn. In this way the men recruited would also include some who were extremely poor, and it was expected that at least some of them would be prepared to join the army, even if only as a

(14) Livius, XXXV, 9.
(15) Livius, *Epit.* XLVI.
(16) Livius, *Epit.* LXVI.
(17) See note 93 of the previous chapter.
(18) *Athenaeum*, N.S. XXVIII (1949), pp. 184-187.

temporary solution to their indigence. The minimum was not abolished completely, because of the Senate's conservative mentality. This was later done by Marius and, as I will demonstrate below, not because of the lack of *assidui*, but in an attempt to overcome the reluctance of the citizens and in the hope of finding volunteers, particularly from that section of the population which owned no property at all. Although there is no actual evidence for this, it is possible that the reduction of the minimum was connected with the distribution of land carried out after Tiberius' death. Unemployed men who became *assidui* through the reduction may have been promised priority in the distribution of land, if they joined the army. Be that as it may, the contention that the reduction was due to a lack of a sufficient number of *assidui* is a modern interpretation which has no basis in the sources and does not accord with the arguments contained in them concerning the reason for the abolition of the minimum by Marius.

The speech made by the censor, Q. Metellus Macedonicus, in 131, about marriage and procreation, may, at first glance, seem to support the argument that there was a dearth of *assidui*, but both its form and content must be carefully examined in this connection. The sources for this speech are Livy's *Epitome* (19), Suetonius (20), and Gellius (21). In Livy we read : "*Q. Metellus censor censuit, ut cogerentur omnes ducere uxores liberorum creandorum causa. Extat oratio eius, quam Augustus Caesar, cum de maritandis ordinibus ageret, uelut in haec tempora scriptam in senatu recitauit*. Suetonius writes : *Etiam libros totos et senatui recitauit et populo notos per edictum saepe fecit, ut orationes Q. Metelli 'de Prole Augenda'*..." Gellius quotes a passage from the speech made by Q. Metellus Numidicus, when he was Censor. A man of this name was Censor in 102 B.C. but the *communis opinio* is that Gellius made a mistake and should have written Macedonius instead of Numidicus (22). Berger successfully refutes Rolf's (23) claims, adding new evidence to prove that the opinion of the majority is indeed correct (24).

The quotations from the speech are as follows : "*Si sine uxore pati possemus quirites, omnes ea molestia careremus, set quoniam ita natura*

(19) *Epit.* LIX.

(20) *Augustus*, 89.

(21) *Noc. Att.*, 1, 6, 1 ff.

(22) For a bibliography of authors who contend that Gellius was mistaken see : A. Berger, *Note on Gellius, N.A., 1, 6*, in *Aj. Ph.*, 67 (1946), p. 323, n. 16.

(23) Rolf's arguments can be found in : *The Attic Nights of Aulus Gellius*, The Loeb Classical Library, Vol. 1, p. 30, n. 1.

(24) *Op. cit.*, p. 325 ff.

tradidit, ut ne cum illis satis commode, nec sine illis ullo modo uiui possit saluti perpetuae potius quam breui uoluptati consulendum est. And the second quotation is : *Di immortales plurimum possunt, sed non plus uelle nobis debent quam parentes. At parentes, si pergunt liberi errare, bonis exheredant. Quid ergo nos ab immortalibus dissimile ius expectemus, nisi malis rationibus finem faciamus? Is demum deos propitios esse aecum est, qui sibi aduersarii non sunt. Dii immortales uirtutem adprobare, non adhibere debent*".

No conclusions can be drawn about the problem under discussion from Gellius' account of the argument about Metellus Macedonicus' speech, since the participants were of Gellius' own generation and their words flowed spontaneously in the course of conversation. They do not constitute serious evidence concerning the Censor's objectives and intentions, and consequently there is no point in quoting them.

It is evident, therefore, that the sources for Q. Metellus Macedonicus' speech make no mention whatsoever of a dearth of men for military purposes, nor of any fear that such a shortage might arise. Suetonius, who refers to the title of the speech *de Prole Augenda* ('About bringing forth children'), states only that Augustus read it out in full before the Senate. It is quite clear that Augustus did this within the framework of his efforts to convince the Senate of the urgency of legislation concerning the problem of marriage. But was it because he was faced with a lack of military manpower that he proposed the *Lex Julia de maritandis ordinibus*, which was passed in the year 17 B.C.? Moreover, if Metellus' speech emphasized this aspect, could Augustus have used it in order to convince others that the law he proposed was necessary? It is obvious that this cannot have been the case. Augustus dissolved thirty legions so that his army comprised only twenty-eight legions, i.e. less than 150,000 men. He also had at his command a reserve of over four million citizens. Had Metullus' speech given prominence to the lack of manpower and stressed the need to establish families in order to provide sufficient candidates for the legions, Augustus could not have read it out in full in the Senate. He could of course have omitted a passage of this kind in the speech, and Suetonius could have erred when he wrote that it was read out *uerbatim* before the Senate. The sources do indeed refer to the necessity of procreation, but this need not necessarily reflect a concern that the numbers of *assidui* would not be adequate for military requirements. As is well known, Augustus introduced legislation concerning marriage in order to raise the moral standards of Roman society. Livy reports that Augustus read Metellus' speech out in the Senate as if it had been written by a contemporary : "*Extat oratio eius quam Augustus Caesare, cum de maritandis ordinibus ageret, uelut in haec tempora scriptam in senatu recitauit*". This would indicate that the content of the speech suited Augustus' situation. It is almost certain, therefore, that the purpose of the speech was to bring about moral reform and social regeneration by marriage. This intention can in fact be found in quotations from the speech cited by Gellius, such as, first : *Saluti perpetuae potius quam breui uoluptati consulendum est.* This sentence is not to be interpreted as meaning that the individual should prefer the good of the nation as a whole to his own momentary pleasure, but that the individual should act with moderation, taking thought for his long-term good.

It is futile to conclude from the argument about the speech conducted during Gellius' time that the issue at stake was the good of the state (25), since this argument took place approximately two hundred and fifty years after the speech was made. The second quotation states that the gods want people to became parents, *Di immortales ... non plus uelle nobis debent quam parentes*, from which it can be understood that not having a family is a moral fault. Whereas the raising of children is *uirtus*. No mention is made in the quotations of procreation and raising a family being urgently needed for national security. The selected passages quoted by Gellius, Livy's comment that the speech was read as if it had been written in Augustus' time and Suetonius' statement that the speech was read out in full before the Senate, all provide strong evidence in support of the contention that the object of the speech was to reform Roman society and not necessarily to encourage the Roman populace to produce children in order to supply sufficient soldiers.

There are also other reasons for assuming that Metellus' aim was not the creation of soldiers. As has been stated above, the Censor made his speech two years after Tiberius Gracchus' tribuneship. It is obvious that he was addressing the Roman populace of the city and not the Roman citizens who resided throughout Italy, in Cisalpine Gaul, in the municipia and other places, not those Roman citizens who had already benefitted from the distribution of land by the Gracchan commission. He did not even address himself principally to those who were likely to receive land in the future, since he doubtless knew that, as far as the rural inhabitants were concerned, the enticements were limited and they were certainly likely to marry in any case. He appealed primarily to the masses living in

(25) BERGER, *op. cit.*, p. 321, n. 5.

Rome and certain to remain there. This multitude was similar in mentality to the population which had been reluctant to be recruited in 151 B.C., and also in 138 B.C. apparently, and in order to carry favour with which, it seems, the Senate had passed a law in 140 B.C. forbidding more than one recruitment to be held each year (these events will be discussed at greater length later in this chapter). The question then arises whether procreation would in fact solve the problem of recruitment among those who were averse to joining the army, since the children would undoubtedly be influenced by their parents' attitude. Some of this populace was unemployed and therefore belonged to the propertyless class ; thus, the Censor must surely have realised that the procreation of children by the *capite censi* would not increase the number of *assidui*.

In short, it may well be that, seeing how Roman society was degenerating, as evidenced by its pursuit of momentary pleasures and reluctance to establish families, the Censor aspired to putting an end to these trends in the same way as Augustus had probably tried to do among the aristocracy. It is also possible that he wished to stop the beginning of the process of a decline in the number of *assidui*. On the other hand, it can hardly be supposed that Q. Metellus sought to solve the problems of recruitment in Rome, which were primarily moral ones (as I shall try to show later on in this chapter), by increasing the birth rate, although he might have believed that social reform would lead to a greater willingness to join the army.

Laelius' proposal to distribute land (26) is also used as evidence for the dearth of *assidui*. It would, however, be pointless to conclude from the one extant sentence on this subject that Laelius wanted to prevent a demographic decline or increase the manpower potential for service in the legions. It can just as well be assumed that he wanted to free Rome of the oppressive burden of the urban masses. His motive might conceivably have been the purely social one of improving the situation of people who had no home other than the streets of the city. Whatever the case, Plutarch does not state explicitly what moved him to propose his plan.

The passage (27) concerning rewards for procreation cannot be used as evidence that there was a steep drop in the birth rate, because the text makes it clear that these rewards had already been introduced previously. It is true that Scipio Aemilianus' complaint, made in 142 B.C. when he was Censor, that couples were obtaining benefits through adopting

(26) Plut., *Ti. Gracch.*, 8.
(27) Gellius, *Noc. Att.*, V, 19, 15-16.

children may indicate that there were childless marriages. There is, however, no way of ascertaining the extent of this phenomenon. It seems unlikely that it was of epidemic proportions, but there were enough instances for the Censor, Scipio, to denounce the practice. Furthermore, the adopting parents may have wished to benefit from the advantages bestowed on large families, and therefore have adopted children in addition to their own.

The claim made in the Senate in 134 B.C. that Italy would be drained of its men if Scipio were allowed to mobilise soldiers before his departure for Spain ([28]) was a demagogic one which undoubtedly did not reflect Italy's demographic situation. The Senate's refusal to allow Scipio to raise soldiers must be considered in the light of its hostility towards him and the general reluctance of people to mobilise for the war in Spain. As is known, the Senate did not even allocate Scipio any funds, but this does not mean that the funds for financing his expenses were not available. Moreover, a force of four thousand men, the force which Scipio managed to raise from among his own supporters, would certainly not have left Italy without men.

The recruitment of youths of less than seventeen, a practice which Gaius Gracchus had wished to put an end to ([29]), gives some indication of the lengths to which the Senate went in order to overcome the shortage of soldiers, but the reason for this shortage still remains unclear. The fact that Gaius tried to put an end to the practice indicates that it persisted until his tribuneship, i.e. even after land had been distributed to a large number of people and the minimal amount of property had been reduced to 1,500 *asses*.

Although the number of *assidui* increased considerably the authorities still required the recruitment of youngsters. It is apparent, therefore, that the shortage of *assidui* was not the cause. The question also arises as to the manner in which these boys were recruited. They were obviously not kidnapped, since the Senate could not have allowed itself to adopt methods of this nature, which would unquestionably have led to widespread unrest. Even the authorities could not have forced the youngsters to obey a recruitment order which was illegal, unless permission had been obtained from their father. These boys may, however, have been their father's *uicarii*, i.e. they served instead of him. The fact that young boys were recruited need not necessarily indicate a

(28) PLUT., *Apophth., Scrip. Min.*, 15.
(29) PLUT., *C. Gracch.*, 5.

shortage of *assidui* : il may well constitute additional evidence for the aversion to military service.

b) The Difficulties of Recruitment

Now that we have shown that there is no real evidence for a shortage of *assidui*, one basic fact should be noted, namely, that from the outbreak of the third Macedonian war until Tiberius' tribuneship, all the instances known to us of the Roman authorities' recruiting difficulties point to the Roman citizens' unwillingness to join the army, rather than to any scarcity of men. It can even be observed that with the passage of time the Senate lost the ability to solve this problem, was drawn after the mood of the Roman populace and even decided its recruitment policy in accordance with this mood.

The first symptom of a lack of enthusiasm for military service was revealed at the time of the third Macedonian war. In 171 B.C. twenty-three officers who were, according to Livy, of the rank of *primus-pilum* (30), refused to be mobilised. They agreed to join the army only on condition that their rank was maintained, and were persuaded to waive this stipulation only after a speech by Sp. Ligustinus, who was of the same rank (31). This was a demonstration of the lack of enthusiasm shown by officers for serving in the legions. It should be noted that, as their rank indicates, during their previous service these officers had served as an example to the rank and file. On the other hand, it is clear that their refusal was not the outcome of deep-rooted opposition to military service, since the speech of their comrade was sufficient to make them change their minds. The case itself was not serious, but it marked the beginning of an increasingly grave development. Two years later the Consuls of 169 B.C. claimed that they were unable to raise men for the war. Their accusation that the *iuniores* were refusing to respond to the recruitment order, *iuniores non responderent*, was answered by two Praetors who claimed that it was not difficult for Consuls to recruit men, but only for Consuls with political ambitions, *non consulibus sed ambitiosis consulibus dilectum difficilem esse*, adding that the Consuls did not recruit men who refused to join up, *neminem inuitum militem ab iis fieri*. At the Praetor's suggestion

(30) Their refusal may have been due to the fact that they had been deprived of their rank, but this also indicates a lack of enthusiasm for military service and the failure to regard it as a supreme vocation.

(31) Livius, XLII, 32-35.

the recruitment was transferred to them (32), and they carried it out successfully within eleven days (33). This incident is instructive, since it indicates not only that there was widespread unwillingness to enlist (which was apparently the outcome of the hardships of the campaign since in 171 B.C. there had been considerable volunteering because of the expectations of booty) (34), but also that in that year the question of recruitment had already acquired political significance in Rome. This significance found expression in the Consul's attempts to bolster their position by appeasing the populace. On the other hand, it is obvious that the political importance of recruitment at this time was slight since the Senate did not recoil from taking a firm stand against the masses, and the Consuls found themselves humiliated in consequence.

However, the fact that the disinclination to join up was a matter of concern is evident from the Censors' addition to the regular oath taken at the census of a special oath in which the individual who was of military age undertook to report for recruitment on the appointed day (35). This measure adopted by the Roman authorities provides an indication of their mentality. No attempt was made to use bureaucratic measures to prevent the recurrence of this phenomenon, and in effect no long-term approach was adopted, since the easier solution of relying on the efficacy of the oath was preferred. This approach would have suited a patriarchal society, but Rome had started ceasing to be such, and no attempt was made to adapt to contemporary reality. And indeed, eighteen years later the oath had become meaningless. In 151 B.C. there was a crisis in Rome centring on the question of recruitment. Although the crisis was short-lived, its character, as reported by Polybius, was such as Rome had never previously known. Simple soldiers, legates and tribunes, i.e. all the ranks of the Roman army, refused to mobilise for fear of the Celtiberic enemy, against whom they were to be sent to fight. Although the crisis cannot have been very grave, since Scipio Aemilianus' personal example was sufficient to persuade the men to change their minds, it does nevertheless reflect the mood of the Roman public, not only in the lower social strata but also in the senatorial class, whose young men served as military tribunes. Polybius gives the following description of the crisis (36) : it arose

(32) Livius, XLIII, 14.
(33) Livius, XLIII, 15.
(34) Livius, XLII, 32.
(35) Livius, XLIII, 14.
(36) Polybius, XXXV, 4.

as a result of the rumours disseminated by Quintus Fulvius Nobilior, the previous commander in Spain, and his associates about the ceaseless battles, the heavy losses amongst the Roman troops, and the heroism of the Celtiberians. When the Roman commander of that year, Marcellus, was afraid to continue the campaign, panic seized the soldiers and their fathers claimed that they had never witnessed anything comparable. The fear went so deep that the military tribunes, the legates and the ordinary soldiers refused to join up, and, worst of all, there was widespread evasion of mobilisation on grounds whose veracity it was "unseemly and impossible" to examine.

Livy [37] and Orosius [38] describe similar developments, though with greater brevity. Both recount the fear of the war in Spain which gripped the young men of Rome, as a result of which neither soldiers, legates or military tribunes were prepared to serve in the army. Livy also reports, in the same passage, that during these events the popular tribunes threw the Consuls into prison, because they refused to release their comrades from military service. This means that the scourge of military evasion had spread to high quarters too, since even the popular tribunes were prepared to aid and abet it. Thus the phenomenon that first appeared in 169 B.C. repeated itself, though this time with greater severity. Whereas, in the first instance, the Senate could adopt a firm stand and cope with the matter, this time, so Polybius writes, the Senate was helpless. The opposition of the masses in 151 B.C. appears to have been stronger, and their political weight in that year must have been greater. Nevertheless, Scipio Aemilianus' personal charisma sufficed to alter the prevailing mood. This incident also demonstrates that it was not men that Rome lacked, but men who were willing to fight.

In connection with Fabius Maximus Aemilianus' departure for Spain in 145 B.C., Appian notes [39] that this Consul was granted the authority to recruit soldiers for his military needs, but that he did not call up veterans who had returned from North Africa, Macedonia and Greece, being compelled to take raw youths who had had no experience of battle. From these he formed two legions. There can be no doubt that Fabius, who was embarking on an extremely dangerous mission in Spain and would be forced to confront the Lusitanian military genius, Viriatus [40], only

(37) *Epit.* 48.
(38) IV, 21, 1.
(39) *Iber.*, 15.
(40) Livius, *Epit.* LII.

reluctantly forewent the experienced soldiers, and in particular those who had fought under Scipio Aemilianus and must have received first-class training. And indeed, he was obliged to devote considerable time and attention to training and disciplining his soldiers (41). He rightly refrained from encountering his great rival, and throughout his first year as Governor of Spain did not engage in battle with him. His achievements during that year were minimal (42). Appian obviously dwelt on the question of mobilisation in order to explain why Fabius' first year as Governor was not marked by any achievements. This episode leads us to conclude that purely military considerations were sacrified to internal political considerations in Rome. The Senate refused to enforce the mobilisation of the veterans, despite the fact that this was essential. It was not prepared to contend with the veterans' unwillingness to continue fighting in a particularly dangerous and unrewarding spot, and displayed the same weakness as in 151 B.C., although in the present case there was moral justification for the evasion. If, however, the basic problem at that time had been a shortage of men, it seems likely that the Senate would have made an effort to persuade the veterans to continue serving in the army. The fact that no pressure was exerted indicates that the problem of numbers did not exist. The Senate was not faced with the dilemma of trying to find sufficient men.

In 140 B.C. Appius Claudius Pulcher initiated a law which forbade conducting two recruitments in one year (43). The background to this legislation and Appius Claudius' intentions are not known to us, but it is clear that the object of the law was to prevent two recruitments in one year. This suggests that technically this could be done quite easily, since it was necessary to take legal steps to prevent it. The legislation implies, therefore, that there was no dearth of men. On the other hand, it is reasonable to assume that the law was introduced with an eye to the alignment of internal political forces at Rome and against the background of the continuing war in Spain. The approval of the proposal by the Senate as a preliminary step taken before its approval by the popular assembly shows that, as regards recruitment, the Senate had for the first time adopted an unequivocal long-term policy. Henceforth the Senate was

(41) Vell. Paterc., II, 5, 3.

(42) App., *Iber.*, 65, reports that, when he went to Gades, an officer under his command was beaten by Viriatus. A year later, however, in 145 B.C., he defeated Viriatus and caused him losses.

(43) Livius, *Epit.*, LIV.

prepared to limit and even prevent recruitment, even when military needs made it essential. Clearly, only the pressure exerted by political forces within Rome forced the Senate to clarify its policy on the issue of recruitment. Its weakness in confronting the populace in 151 B.C. and 145 B.C. explains the background to the law, evincing the Senate's inability to oppose the temper of the Roman populace, even to the extent of its not being prepared to grapple with a problem fraught with military dangers. Sallust claims, that after the destruction of Carthage, the populace began to substitute licentiousness for liberty (44). It is difficult to ascertain precisely what is meant by this, but it may well refer to the problem of reçruitment, hinting at the opposition of the mob. It would come as no surprise were the law found to reflect the Senate's surrender to the pressures of the populace, which was already deeply infected with unwillingness to join the army.

In 138 B.C. a number of events occurred which were connected with military service. Livy relates that a soldier named Gaius Matienus was accused before the people's popular tribunes of deserting from the army in Spain ; he was found guilty, flogged and sold into slavery (45). This incident served as a healthy example to the soldiers, in Livy's opinion. Elsewhere he reports additional cases of deserters who were flogged and sold into slavery in that year (46). These revelations indicate that it was necessary to deter the new recruits from deserting. Livy also recounts that in that year the popular tribunes threw the Consuls into prison because they would not allow each tribune to furnish ten men with an exemption from military service (47). This fact clearly shows that recruits sought ways of obtaining their release and that there were even some, almost certainly sons of noble families, that managed to gain the assistance of the tribunes, who were prepared to help in the evasion of military service. This phenomenon had in fact occurred already in the year 151, at the time of the recruitment crisis, but its recurrence indicates that it had become habitual.

All the instances cited above indicate that the atmosphere in Rome was one of unwillingness to join the army. The basic reason for this was the

(44) *B.J.*, XLI.

(45) *Epit.*, LV.

(46) Livius, *Epit.* LV ; Frontinus, *Strategemata*, IV, 1, 20.

(47) *Epit.*, LV. For the episode of imprisonment of the Consuls see also : Cic., *De Leg.*, III, 20.

hardships of the war in Spain [48]. The aversion to recruitment was not restricted to the simple people, but also extended to the upper class. The Senate, which was the authority that decided matters of policy, found no way of grappling positively with this state of affairs and simply came to terms with reality and the prevailing spirit. Because of its self-assurance after the various victories during the second century B.C. the military alertness by which it had been distinguished until the destruction of Carthage was dulled. The Senate began to take military chances which cannot be defined as calculated risks, but rather as deriving from a certain lassitude or psychological inability to seek solutions to problems. None of the examples, however, provide evidence of a shortage of *assidui*.

Marius' reform of mobilisation and the decline of mobilisation in Rome during the first century B.C. also support our thesis. Brunt maintains that the lack of *assidui* induced Marius to mobilise the propertyless classes to fill the ranks of the legions [49]. The classical sources, however, contain no indication that this contention is correct.

In a speech which Sallust puts into Marius' mouth, the latter makes the following statement [50] : "*Neque me fallit quantum cum maxumo beneficio uostro negoti sustineam. Bellum parare simul, et aerario parcere, cogere ad militiam eos quos nolis offendere ... quirites asperius est*". This part of the speech makes it clear that the problem of recruitment with which Marius had to contend was that of enlisting men who were unwilling to serve in the army. The words quoted above are the only ones in the entire speech which refer to the difficulties of recruitment and they contain no allusion to a lack of *assidui*, i.e. of men who could legally be recruited. At the end of the passage quoted, we read that the problem was a serious one, *asperius est*, in which case, how did Marius cope with it? Or is there perhaps an element of deception in this statement, since by mobilising the *capite censi*, who flocked to the legions of their own free will, Marius overcame the problem with ease?

In paragraph 84 Sallust writes : "*interim quae bello opus erant prima habere postulare legionibus supplementum, auxilia a populis et regibus arcessere, praeterea ex Latio sociisque fortissimum quemque, plerosque*

(48) As I have demonstrated, most of the instance of reluctance to join the army were connected with the war in Spain. The war itself however, was not the sole reason for this.

(49) *Op. cit.*, p. 407. The paucity of men who could be mobilised as a factor in Marius' reform is also mentioned in : G. Bloch, *M. Aemilius Scaurus*, Paris, 1909, p. 47.

(50) *B.J.*, 85, 3.

militiae paucos fama cognitos accire et ambiundo cogere homines emeritis stipendiis secum proficisci. Neque illi senatus quamquam aduorsus erat, de ullo negotio abnuere audebat. Ceterum supplementum etiam leatus decreuerat, quia neque plebi militia uolenti putabatur, et Marius aut belli usum aut studia uolgi amissurus, sed ea res frustra sperata, tanta lubido cum Mario eundi plerosque inuaserat. Sese quisque praeda locupletem fore, uictorem domum rediturum, alia huiuscemodi animis trahebant".

This important passage reveals that Marius was interested in mobilising brave soldiers with battle experience, and that he sought them throughout Latium. It is highly probable that there were very few in Rome itself and that this is why he was obliged to look for them in Latium. There cannot have been many there either, since he attempted to persuade veterans who had completed their terms of service, *homines emeritis stipendiis*, to accompany him to North Africa. This painstaking search justifies the statement attributed by Sallust to Marius, to the effect that the mobilisation of troops was a laborious task for him. From this passage we also learn that there was a general feeling in Rome that the populace did not want to serve in the army. The Senate willingly acceded to Marius' request to carry out an enlistment of soldiers, in the hope that this would serve to deprive him of the basis of his power. It was expected that he would lose the support of the masses, since the plebeians had no desire to serve in the army, *quia neque plebi militia uolenti putabatur*.

The two passages quoted indicate that Marius' problem was qualitative rather than quantitative. It was not the dearth of men which concerned him, but the lack of experienced and suitable soldiers. The prevailing general atmosphere in Rome of reluctance to enlist and serve in the army undoubtedly constituted the root of the problem, since a soldier who had been recruited against his will would hardly have made a good soldier. Marius tried, therefore, to mobilise men who were known as good soldiers, and also attempted to do this without resorting to coercion. In the passage cited, Sallust relates that the Senate's hope that Marius would lose the support of the Plebeians because of their unwillingness to be recruited was not fulfilled, for men enlisted voluntarily and enthusiastically. Sallust does not explain at this juncture how Marius succeeded in attracting men to the army, limiting himself to the general explanation that "each man imagined to himself that he would grow rich through booty". There is no doubt that this explanation is only partial and the reform of the mobilisation system also played a part in this success.

What are the reasons mentioned by the ancient sources for the reform ?

Exuperantius»([51]) provides an account which is irrelevant to our purposes. He states that the change in the method of mobilisation was introduced because, *Cum publico detrimento populo gratiam redderet, a quo speratos honores acceperat*. In other words, because of the mobilisation of the *capite censi*, Marius would receive *speratos honores*, i.e. a craving for honour impelled him to take this step. Valerius Maximus ([52]) maintains that the reason for the reform was Marius' awareness of the fact that he was *homo nouus*, and his fear of being mocked by the army in consequence. He accordingly considered it necessary to abolish the old recruitment system : *Ne talis notae contagio ad ipsius quoque gloriae subgillationum penetraret*.

In Sallust we find the following passage ([53]) : *Ipse interea milites scribere non more maiorum, neque ex classibus sed uti cuiusque lubido erat, capite censos plerosque. Id factum alii inopia bonorum, alii per ambitionem consulis memorabant quod ab eo genere celebratus auctusque erat*...

Two explanations are given here ; the first is *inopia bonorum*, and the second is Marius' personal ambition for fame and glory. For our purposes it is important to understand the significance of the words *inopia bonorum*. From Gabba's study ([54]), it can be understood that, in his opinion, *inopia bonorum* is a shortage of *assidui*, although he takes care not to say this explicitly. He claims that in 107 B.C. the scarcity of manpower was acute, as a result of the losses suffered by the Roman army at Noricum in 113 B.C. and in Gaul in 107 B.C. It is his opinion that the advantage gained by reducing the property minimum to 1,500 *asses* had been obliterated. The request to the allies to send military reinforcements also testifies that there was a shortage of manpower, and that this was the reason for the mobilisation of the *capite censi*. Brunt states explicitly that *inopia bonorum* is the shortage of *assidui* ([55]). From the information given by Sallust, however, it is perfectly apparent that it was the qualitative factor which concerned Marius and not the quantitative one. When looked at in this light, *boni* means good soldiers rather than *assidui*. Furthermore, Sallust would not tend to use the term *boni* to denote the *assidui*, since *boni* was also a class appellation, The *optimates*, who considered themselves a select elite, applied this term to themselves.

(51) Opusc. 2.
(52) II, 3, 1.
(53) *B.J.*, 86.
(54) *Athenaeum*, 1949, pp. 199-200.
(55) *Op. cit.*, p. 407.

It hardly seems likely, therefore, that Sallust, the *popularis*, would use this appellation of the *assidui*, i.e. would make a qualitative distinction between the poor of Rome who possessed 1,500 *asses* and those who did not own such a paltry sum (as I shall show later on in this chapter), asserting that the former were *boni* and the latter were not. Had Sallust belonged to the *optimates* this would have been reasonable ; but he was a *popularis*, and it is unreasonable to assume that he would adopt a negative attitude towards that section of the populace which participated in the popular assembly and supported his faction, simply because it did not possess that small amount of money. It is unrealistic to assume that he made a distinction between *assidui* and *capite censi* because of a purely formal matter which was of no significance for many of the *assidui*. Furthermore, it can hardly be assumed that Sallust's use of the term *inopia bonorum* referred to a scarcity of men with property (*boni*-property) who were liable for recruitment. The minimum of 1,500 *asses* could not possibly have been defined as *boni*, since, as stated above, this was a very small sum. There can be no doubt that the word *boni* should be interpreted literally as 'good', i.e. good soldiers. *Inopia bonorum* means, therefore, a shortage of good soldiers. Marius opened the ranks of the legion to the *capite censi* and used no coercion to mobilise those who were willing to join, hoping that they would prove to be good soldiers. This interpretation is supported by Quintilian. He stresses the fact that the qualitative factor induced Marius to mobilise the *capite censi* : *Vel ex eo manifestum est quod cum scires non ex censu esse uirtutem* (56). Thus, there is no indication in the sources that the shortage of *assidui* was the reason which impelled Marius to mobilise them.

One of the arguments used to support the claim that there really was a scarcity of *assidui* in 107 B.C. is the fact that, in 109 B.C., M. Iunius Silanus annulled the laws reducing the number of years of military service. However, the validity of this argument is refuted by Marius' appeal to the veterans, which was made because he wanted his soldiers to be courageous and experienced and not because there was a shortage of men. The reluctance of the populace to join the army and the desire to raise the standard of the soldiers serving in the legions may well have been the reasons for Silanus' decision to annul the laws. In 107 B.C. Marius mobilised only five thousand soldiers (57), and it is absurd to claim that in

(56) *Decl.*, III, 5.
(57) BRUNT, *op. cit.*, p. 430.

Rome and Latium there were not five thousand men with the trivial sum of 1,500 *asses*. Cicero's contention that, in claiming that there were not two thousand propertied men in the state Philippus was engaging in demagoguery, must be accepted (58). Moreover, it seems improbable that Philippus was referring to the *assidui* when he maintained that *non esse in ciuitate duo milia hominum qui rem haberent*. Could a man who possessed 1,500 *asses* be considered someone *qui rem haberet*?

Obviously the inclusion of the *capite censi* in the legions and the granting of citizenship to all Italy increased the potential manpower of the army considerably. It can, therefore, be stated unequivocally that after 90 B.C. there was no numerical lack of men who could be enlisted for the legions. An interesting and conspicuous fact, which has already been noted by Brunt, is that at that period there were very few recruitments in Rome (59), most of them being conducted in the other parts of Italy. Brunt explains this by the fact that the inhabitants of Rome, including the proletariat, did not want to be mobilised. It might be added that since, sources of manpower existed in other regions, the Roman populace was not forced to join the army except in cases of emergency. This state of affairs continued during the Imperial era too. Forni has computed tables showing that from the time of Augustus down to that of Diocletian, soldiers for the legions were not enlisted in Rome (60), even though Rome was a densely populated metropolis. This fact constitutes conclusive evidence that the principal problem of recruitment in the city of Rome itself, as far as the Gracchi were concerned, was the unwillingness of the populace there to join the army, and not the lack of *assidui*.

The reluctance to enlist in the army was not restricted to the city of Rome alone. Brunt has shown convincingly that during the first century B.C. mobilisation was usually carried out by coercion (61). The fact that even when the recruitments were small they were compulsory is particularly interesting. Thus, for example, in the year 64 B.C. Murena raised a *supplementum* (i.e. a small number of men), for three legions, but he was nevertheless forced to coerce them into enlisting (62). Mobilisation was not popular, and men refrained from enlisting even though

(58) Cic., *De Off.*, II, 21, 73.

(59) *The Army and the Land in the Roman Revolution*, in *J.R.S.*, LII (1962), p. 74.

(60) Forni, *Il reclutamento delle legioni da Augusto a Diocleziano*, Roma, 1953, p. 159 ff.

(61) *Op. cit.*, p. 408 ff.

(62) Cic., *Pro Mur.*, 42 ; Brunt, *op. cit.*, pp. 409-410. See also, Brunt, *op. cit.*, p. 635 ff.

considerable spoils were anticipated. Before leaving for Parthia, Crassus was obliged to enlist his soldiers by coercion (63), despite the fact that there were great prospects that tremendous booty would be taken. During the Imperial era soldiers were not enlisted in republican Italy apart from Umbria and Etruria, where limited recruitments were conducted (64). This is partially explained by the population's reluctance to enlist, as is reflected in the writings of Velleius Paterculus (65), who reports that, until Tiberius' time, the recruitments inspired great fear in the population, and it is known that Tiberius initiated the policy of transferring the burden of recruitment from the inhabitants of Italy to Roman citizens in the provinces (66). Thus, the lack of enthusiasm for military service, as revealed in the first century B.C. as well as during the Imperial period, provides further evidence for the contention that the core of the problem, prior to Tiberius Gracchus' term of office, was the general unwillingness to enlist and not a shortage of *assidui*.

c) The Demography of the *assidvi*

Having discussed the recruitment problems deriving from the citizens' reluctance to enlist, we will now examine the demographic situation of the *assidui* class. The census figure provides the key to this question. If this figure does not include the *capite censi*, as I have attempted to prove above, then the number of *assidui* was more than 300,000 (67). Since at that time an average of less than 40,000 men served in the legions (68), there was certainly no shortage of *assidui*. Although before Tiberius Gracchus' tribuneship there was a decline in the census figures, this was slight and far from constituting a danger to Roman manpower potential. Since, however, it is not absolutely certain that the *capite censi* were not included in the census figures, this assumption will not serve as the sole basis of our contention. If we proceed on the opposite assumption that the *capite censi* were included in the census figure, the number of *assidui* will be obtained by deducting the number of *capite censi* from the total. Our task is, therefore, to attempt to make a rough estimate of the size of the proletariat before Tiberius Gracchus' appearance on the political scene.

(63) Dio, XXXIX, 39, 1. The mobilisation was conducted by Pompey and Crassus.
(64) Forni, *op. cit.*, p. 159 ff.
(65) II, 130, 2.
(66) Tac., *Ann.*, IV, 4.
(67) Livius, *Per.* LVI.
(68) Brunt, *op. cit.*, pp. 429 and 432.

It is possible to state unequivocally that, at the beginning of the second century B.C., the proletariat was not very large. As is well known, the members of this class served in the navy, but in 190 B.C. there were not enough men to provide the necessary manpower, so that the inhabitants of the maritime colonies were compelled to join the navy (69), and even the *Libertini* were impressed into this service (70). Since thirty thousand Roman citizens and allies served in the navy (71), it is evident that the proletariat was limited in size. The numerical smallness of the proletariat was probably the result of the land settlement activities of 232 B.C., the settling of 50,000 veterans in Samnium and Apuleia in 200 B.C. and various colonizing operations before and after the Second Punic War. It can be assumed that, during the first half of the second century B.C., the numbers of the proletariat did not increase significantly since, as will be demonstrated below, dispossession was not on a large scale and the proletariat was directed to new areas of settlement. Toynbee was right in observing (72) that, until 167 B.C. at least, the *Lex de modo agrorum*, limiting land that could be owned to 500 *iugera*, was respected. The extant fragment of Cato's speech : *Ecqua tamen lex est acerba quae dicat, si quis plus quingenta iugera habere uoluerit tanta poena esto... Atque nos omnia plura habere uolumus, et id nobis impune est* (73), shows that the law was a strict one, and even though people wanted to violate it they did not do so, and no punishment could be incurred for the thought unaccompanied by the deed (74). This makes it clear that, at least until 167 B.C., the expansion of the *latifundia* and the dispossession of the citizens was not widespread. The plight of the proletariat which had come into being by this date was alleviated by colonizing and settlement activities, which continued uninterruptedly until 173 B.C. and even afterwards (75).

(69) Livius, XXXVI, 3.

(70) Livius, XXXVI, 2.

(71) Brunt, *op. cit.*, p. 425.

(72) *Op. cit.*, Vol. II, p. 555.

(73) Quoted in Gellius, VI, 3, 37.

(74) This is stated clearly at the end of the passage quoted. About the view that the small peasant was surviving on a large scale, at least in Cato's days, that means till the middle of the second century B.C. See : *Aufstieg und Niedergang der römischer Welt*, Berlin, 1970, p. 671 (J. Vogt, E. Badian).

(75) The possibility that lands were distributed according to the *assignatio viritim* system in Cisalpine Gaul after 173 B.C. should not be disregarded. It may well be that because of the limited number of sources no information concerning this has been preserved. In 169 B.C. Aquileia was reinforced by 1,500 new settlers (Livius, XLIII, 17), in 168 B.C. Forum Licinii was founded and in 157 Auximum, which was a Roman colony of the Latin type, was established.

Sallust claims that the rift within the Roman nation began with the destruction of Carthage, i.e. in the year 146 B.C., and that one of its characteristic features was the eviction of the poor from their land (76). Although much in this passage of Sallust's is inaccurate and the process of sequestration certainly began before 146 B.C., as is demonstrated by Appian (77) and Plutarch (78), it can nevertheless be supposed that it was at approximately that time that the *Lex de modo agrorum* began to be disregarded and dispossession became extensive. Possible Sallust's intention was not to say that there had not been any expropriation of land before the destruction of Carthage, but that from that time on it had a momentous effect on Rome's internal life. Even if Sallust's contention is not accepted literally, the foregoing indicates that until approximately 146 B.C. the proletariat did not constitute a large section within Roman society.

In his important article (79), Boren has shown that the dispossessed who moved to Rome found employment there in building and public works, which were being conducted on an extensive scale. It seems probable, as I shall demonstrate below, that most of the employed men were not included in the category of the *capite censi* but were *assidui*. It is also possible, although there is no actual evidence of this, that the employment was also directed towards enabling dispossessed persons and the people who voluntarily flocked to Rome to retain the status of *assidui*. The construction work continued as long as money flowed into the city, and began to diminish in extent after 140 B.C. Consequently, it seems reasonable to assume that the number of *capite censi* till that date was not large. This assertion is corroborated by the fact that the poor were also counted among the *assidui* and only paupers and the destitute were included in the category of *capite censi*. As is well known, it was necessary to possess 4,000 *asses* in order to be included among the *assidui*. It has been pointed out above that this minimum was reduced to 1,500 *asses* between 133 and 125 B.C. (80). What, then, was the purchasing power of 4,000 *asses*?

Until the tribuneship of Gaius Gracchus the price of a *modius* of wheat was approximately ten *asses*. An individual person consumed five *modii* a

(76) *B.J.*, 41.
(77) *B.C.*, 1, 7.
(78) *Ti. Gracchus*, 8.
(79) *The Urban Side of the Gracchan Economic Crisis*, in *A.H.R.*, 63 (1958), p. 890 ff.
(80) E. Gabba in *Athenaeum*, N.S. XXVII, 1949, p. 184 ff.

month, i.e. sixty *modii* a year. He thus spent six hundred *asses* a year on wheat. Naturally, the cost of baked bread was somewhat higher. It would not be unreasonable to state that about 4,000 *asses* were required to buy bread for a family of four for a year. Plutarch relates (81) that, in his youth, i.e. around the year 120 B.C., Sulla owned very little property, since his father had left him nothing and he paid three thousand *sestertia* in rent, i.e. 12,000 *asses*. A freed slave paid two thousand *sestertia*, i.e. 8,000 *asses*, as rent for an attic in the same house. Plutarch notes the rent, in order to describe Sulla's impecunious condition as a young man. Even if the rent paid by the freed slave for the attic was higher than the average rent in Rome, it can be said that a Roman whose wage was sufficient to pay for a humble apartment and could barely support himself and his family was an *assiduus*. Even a bachelor who scarcely earned enough to pay for his food and lodging may have been included within this category. Hence, anyone who found reasonably respectable employment was not included among the *capite censi*. Only the unemployment which developed at Rome a few years before the appearance of Tiberius Gracchus on the political scene accelerated the creation of a proletariat. It can be assumed that those few years were not sufficient for an extensive proletariat to have come into being. An idea of its actual size may perhaps be obtained from the fact that in the year 70 B.C. Cicero reported (82) that approximately 200,000 *modii* sufficed to provide the plebeians with inexpensive wheat. Thus the number of people who received this wheat was 40,000 at the most, and this was the number of poor people in Rome at that time. Clearly, there were fewer than this before the tribuneship of Tiberius Gracchus (83).

Having seen that the process of dispossession and the influx of people into Rome did not give rise to a large proletariat, let us now discuss in general terms the distribution of the body of Roman citizens throughout Italy. This will enable us to estimate, if only roughly, the manpower potential of the Roman citizen army. A large reservoir of citizens was concentrated in Cisalpine Gaul and North Italy. There are figures for the

(81) *Sulla*, 1.

(82) *In Verr.*, II, 3, 72.

(83) I accept Brunt's assumption (*op. cit.*, p. 24) that the statement made by Dionysius (VII, 59, 6) to the effect that there were more men without property than with was based on the state of affairs in his own time. In my opinion, during the second half of the first century B.C. the number of poor people increased considerably, and this was reflected by the numbers receiving wheat on the basis of Pompey's list. This was later reduced to half by Julius Caesar, and was restricted to 150,000 men.

population of Latin-type colonies of Roman citizens which were established in this region during the second century B.C. Two colonies of Roman citizens, Mutina and Parma, were established in 183 B.C. in Cisalpine Gaul, on territory belonging to the Boii. Two thousand settlers were sent to each colony (84). In the same year the Roman colony of Saturnia, which was of the new type, was established at Ager Calteranus in Etruria (85). There is no record of the number of settlers there. Two years later the Roman colony of Graviscae, which was also of the new type, was founded in Etruria (86). Livy does not note the number of settlers sent there. In 177 B.C. the Roman colony of Luna was established on the territory of the Apuani, and comprised two thousand settlers (87). In 157 B.C. the Roman colony Auximum, which was of the new type (88), was founded at *ager Picenus*. There is no record of the number of settlers sent there. However, since two thousand people were sent to each of the three Roman colonies of the Latin type, it can be assumed that a similar number of settlers was sent to the three other colonies which were of the same type. There is, therefore, a sound basis for presuming that, prior to Tiberius Gracchus' tribuneship, the number of Roman citizens in these colonies exceeded ten thousand, the vast majority of them being *assidui*. It is known that Mutina (89) and Parma (90) were large cities at the beginning of the Imperial era and that Luna was also prosperous (91). It seems likely, therefore, that they were already expanding and growing in the course of the second century B.C., and that on the eve of Tiberius Gracchus' appearance on the political scene each one comprised more than two thousand citizens.

In the year 232 B.C. Roman citizens settled at *ager Gallicus et Picenus*. T. Frank has stated that, if the units of distribution were of seven *iugera*, it would have been possible to settle sixty thousand persons on that area (92). It does not appear reasonable to conclude that so many settlers were sent by Flaminius, but the census figures provide a basis for assuming that the settlement was a large one (between ten and twenty thousand people were

(84) Livius, XXXIX, 55.
(85) Livius, XXXIX, 55.
(86) Livius, XL, 29.
(87) Livius, XLI, 13.
(88) Vell. Paterc., I, 15.
(89) Strab., V, 1, 11, p. 216 ; P.W., *R.-E.*, I, 31, s.v. *mutina*, col. 941.
(90) Strab., V, 1, 11, p. 216.
(91) Brunt, *op. cit.*, pp. 350-351.
(92) *Economic Survey of Ancient Rome*, 1, Baltimore, 1923, p. 61.

settled there). The census of 233/4 enumerated 270,713 people (93). From Polybius' work it can be inferred that in 225 this number had grown to 325,300 (94). This numerical growth can be explained in part by the conversion of *capite censi* to *assidui* through their settlement, and their consequent inclusion in the census figure cited by Polybius. In 173 B.C. an *assignatio uiritim* was implemented for Roman citizens and Latins in *ager Ligustinus et Gallicus*. Livy, who is the sole source of information about this distribution of land, writes : "*Eodem anno, cum agri Ligustini et Gallici quod bello captum, erat aliquantum uacaret, senatus consultum factum ut is ager uiritim diuideretur.... Diuiserunt dena iugera in singulis, sociis nominis Latini terna*" (95).

This passage informs us that the territory distributed was extensive (96) and that the units of land were small. This means that large numbers of people were settled in these areas. There is plausible conjecture that the Latins became Roman citizens upon being settled (97). It is reasonable, therefore, to suppose that there were very many Roman citizens in these two areas (98). This contention is further supported by the following facts. The losses incurred by the Ligures in the battles were great (99). In 180 B.C. 47,000 Apuani (100), not including women and children, were exiled to Samnium, most of their lands being sequestered (101) and their places taken by Roman citizens (102). The number of Boii killed was also very

(93) LIVIUS, *Epit.* 20.

(94) POLYB., II, 24. See a discussion of this subject in the first chapter of this work.

(95) XLII, 4.

(96) That this was indeed the case see : TIBILETTI, in *Athenaeum*, 1950, p. 207 ; EWINS, in *P.B.S.C.*, 1952, p. 57.

(97) P. A. BRUNT, in *J.R.S.*, 1965, p. 90 ; *Italian Manpower*, p. 168 ; TOYNBEE, Vol. II, p. 153 ; R. E. SMITH, in *J.R.S.*, 1954, p. 18 ff.

(98) This is contended by EWINS, *op. cit.*, p. 60, and TOYNBEE, Vol. II, pp. 149 and 200. The opposite view presented by BRUNT in *Italian Manpower*, p. 193, is not with accord with Livy's text and with other data which will be discussed.

(99) The reported losses amounted to 84,000, but this figure appears to be exaggerated. See : BRUNT, *op. cit.*, p. 188.

(100) LIVIUS, XL, 38-41.

(101) LIVIUS, XL, 38.

(102) BRUNT's claim, presented in *Italian Manpower*, p. 197, that the expulsion of the Apuani from Liguria to Samnium did not result in the settlement of citizens there, but possibly people from Umbria and Etruria and soldiers who had served in the region were brought there, is unacceptable for two reasons. The first is that in describing the *assignatio uiritim* conducted in 173 B.C. LIVY (XLII, 4) refers to the distribution of land in *ager Ligustinus*, and this land could have belonged only to the Apuani. The second is that this region was known for its *fora* and *conciliabula*, which were communities of Roman citizens.

large (103), and Strabo reports that many of them migrated to Bohemia (104). Roman citizens were also settled on their lands, half of which, according to Livy, were expropriated (105). The lands distributed in 173 were those that had been annexed to the Pollia tribe, both in Aemilia (along the Via Aemilia), and in Liguria (106), and were very extensive.

In 172 B.C. the Senate decided to settle the Statielli north of the Po. This tribe had been uprooted from its home as a result of the attack by the consul M. Popilius Laenas (107). Its land was thus taken from it, which meant that in that year additional land south of the Po was available for distribution to Roman citizens. About 20,000 Statielli were slain or exiled (108). This decision was passed by the Senate even though it had previously condemned Popilius Laenas' attack on the Statielli, and branded it as unjust, since it had been launched against a peaceful tribe. Accordingly, it is clear that, on second thoughts, the Senate wanted to take advantage of the opportunity to expropriate new lands, in order to settle Roman citizens in the region.

There is no doubt that public opinion in Rome at that time approved the large-scale implementation of the land-distribution policy. This can be inferred from the declarations of C. Claudius Pulcher, who boasted in 176 that, as a result of his victories, land had been conquered which could be divided up amongst many thousands of people : ... *agrique aliquantum captum qui multis milibus hominum diuidi uiritim posset* (109). This statement, which was undoubtedly unfounded (110), can only be under-

(103) The losses suffered by the Gauls, as reported by Livy, were : 35,000 killed or captured in 200 B.C. (XXX, 21, 7), 35,000 of the Insubres slain in 197 B.C. (XXXII, 30, 11), 40,000 Gauls killed in 196 B.C. (XXXIII, 36, 13), in the same year an entire attacking force of Gauls was completely destroyed, but their number was not given (XXXII, 37, 8). In 195 B.C. 80,000 Boii were slain (XXXIV, 22, 2), in 194 B.C. 10,000 Insubres and Boii were killed (XXXIV, 46, 1), in the same year 11,000 Boii were slain (XXXIV, 47, 8). In 193 B.C. 14,000 Boii were killed (XXXV, 5, 13), and in 191 B.C. 32,000 Boii (XXVI, 38, 6). These figures are undoubtedly exaggerated, and Livy himself relates that Antias, from whom he obtained them, tended to exaggerate (XXXVI, 38, 7). However, even if the losses among the Gauls were only one quarter of those given they still amounted to approximately 50,000.

(104) V, 1, 6, p. 213, and also Pliny, *N.H.*, III, 116.

(105) XXXVI, 39.

(106) See on this subject : U. Ewings, in *P.B.S.R.*, 1955, p. 55, and also U. Ewins, in *P.B.S.R.*, 1952, p. 73 ff.

(107) Livius, XLII, 22.

(108) Livius, XLII, 22.

(109) Livius, XLI, 16, 8.

(110) On this topic see : Toynbee, *op. cit.*, Vol. II, p. 184, and also Brunt, *op. cit.*, p. 188.

stood in the light of its author's desire to win popularity within the Senate and among the Roman people. Polybius reports [111] that he had seen that the Gauls had been driven away from the entire Po valley, except for a few areas at the foot of the Alps. This statement has already been proved to be far from accurate [112], but obviously Polybius had seen extensive areas which were empty of Gauls, and there is no reason to assume that their place was not taken by Roman citizens. It is to be supposed that the settlement of Romans in the region continued also after 173 B.C., particularly since the region was quiet [113], but because of the paucity of the sources we have no information about this. The question then arises, what became of the settler? One scholarly opinion is that *latifundii* did not develop in Cisalpine Gaul [114]. However, Brunt's new assumption that it is highly improbable that the aristocratic government neglected its own interests in Cisalpine Gaul is far more logical. He also surmises that the penetration of men of property was primarily into places where such problems as draining swamps or clearing forests arose, since these activities were beyond the capabilities of the small farmer [115]. Consequently, they entered regions where the *assignatio uiritim* had doubtless not yet been implemented. It can, therefore, be said that most of the small farmers who were settled in Cisalpine Gaul had established themselves there and had not been compelled to leave their homes.

The available data — that the Latin-type colonies of Roman citizens comprised at least ten thousand citizens, that almost fifty thousand Apuani were evacuated, tens of thousands of Ligures and Galii were killed, many Boii were exiled to Bohemia, some twenty thousand Statielli were slain or transferred beyond the Po and that many were settled by Flaminius, in 173 B.C. and in the years which followed, — all this leads to the conclusion that, on the eve of Tiberius Gracchus' tribuneship, the Roman citizens settled on land in Cisalpine Gaul and North Italy most probably numbered tens of thousands.

Another substantial agglomeration of Roman citizens was to be found in the municipia scattered throughout central Italy and Campania. Beloch has suggested that the *ciues sine suffragio* were also included in the census

(111) II, 35.

(112) Brunt, *op. cit.*, p. 197 ; Toynbee, *op. cit.*, II, p. 255.

(113) Tibiletti, in *Athenaeum*, 1950, p. 207.

(114) Mommsen, *G.S.*, V, pp. 123 ff. and 136 ff. ; L. Ruggini, *Economia e società nell'"Italia Annonaria"*, Milan, 1961, p. 24, n. 29 ; Chilver, *op. cit.*, p. 146.

(115) *Op. cit.*, p. 195.

figure ([116]). He has been followed in this by Toynbee ([117]) and Brunt ([118]). Even if this was not the case, as I incline to believe, many *municipia* were *optime iure* before 133 B.C. ([119]), and Brunt maintains that all of them were ([120]). The reference here is to more than forty cities ([121]) but it is quite impossible to estimate their population. The sole exception is Capua, where the number of *iuniores* in 216 B.C. was 34,000 ([122]), and clearly this city cannot serve as an indication, since it was the second largest in Italy. There is no doubt, however, that from the large number of cities we may conclude that their overall population numbered several dozens of thousands. Since it is known that 4,000 men emigrated to Fregellae, an extremely low hypothetical figure of one thousand *assidui* to a *municipium* can be assumed. The overall figure, except of course for the Campania, will be around forty thousand men. However, even if many *municipia* were not *optimo iure* before 133 B.C., it can be confidently asserted that their citizens served in the legions ([123]). In 282 B.C. there was a legion consisting of men from Capua, which was *ciuitas sine suffragio*. It served as a garrison force in Regium that year, called *Legio Campana* ([124]) by Livy and *Octaua legio* by Orosius ([125]). Possibly the legion's disgraceful behaviour at Regium led to the removal of men from *municipia sine suffragio* from the legions, since in 279 B.C. they did not serve in them ([126]). However, excerpts from the writings of Festus made by Paulus indicate that the men from the *municipia sine suffragio* (he mentions Cumae, Acerrae and Atella, which fell into this category) did serve in the legions ([127]). The following passage, which defines *munici-pes* ([128]), indicates it quite clearly, that the reference is to *ciuitates sine suf-fragio*. "*Id genus hominum dicitur, qui cum Romam uenissent neque ciues*

(116) *Klio*, III, p. 471 ff. ; *Bevölkerung*, p. 319.

(117) *Op. cit.*, Vol. I, p. 456.

(118) *Op. cit.*, p. 17 ff.

(119) Toynbee, *op. cit.*, I, p. 403 ff., thinks that the *municipia* of Greater Latium were granted the status of *optimo iure* in 268 B.C., and those south of Rome in 225 B.C. It is known that Fundi Formiae and Arpinum received full citizenship in 188 B.C.

(120) *Op. cit.*, p. 20.

(121) P.W., *R.-E.*, 1, 31, s.v. *municipium*, col. 576 ff.

(122) Livius, XXIII, 5, 15.

(123) Toynbee, *op. cit.*, I, p. 201 ff.

(124) *Epit.* XII and XV.

(125) IV, 3.

(126) This transpires from the description given by Dionysius, XX, 1, of the battle of Asculum.

(127) L. 117, L. 126.

(128) L. 155.

Romani essent. Participes tamen fuerunt omnium rerum ad munus fungendum una cum Romanis ciuibus praeterquam de suffragio ferendo, aut magistratu capiendo sicut fuerunt Fundani, Formiani, Cumani, Lanuuini, Tusculani". There is no concrete reason to suppose that Festus was mistaken. The men of the *municipia* were barred from serving in the legions after 282 B.C., but were again made subject to military service at a later date, possibly some time after the first Punic War, as Beloch argues ([129]), or at some point prior to the Second Punic War, as Brunt opines ([130]).

Certain reserves of Roman citizens were also to be found in Apulia and Samnium. It is known that fifty thousand veterans ([131]) were settled in these areas in 200 B.C., but nothing is known of their fate or that of their descendants. Nevertheless, it can be assumed that several thousand remained there, since Apulia was a fertile region ([132]).

To sum up, the demographic review shows that, apart from Rome, there were two large reservoirs of potential manpower for service in the legions. One was in north Italy, while the other was in the centre and in Campania. Even if the *capite censi* were included in the census figure, there are grounds for assuming that the manpower potential for service in the legions was far greater than the number of men actually serving in them.

Tens of thousands of *assidui* most probably lived in Cisalpine Gaul, north Italy and the *municipia*. The figures given above allow us to sumise that outside Rome there were more than one hundred thousand men available to serve in the legions throughout Italy. (The general impression one gains is that there were more than fifty thousand in Cisalpine Gaul and North Italy, approximately fifty thousand in the *municipia* of central Italy, and about fifty thousand in Campania, Apulia and Samnium.) Since, as we have seen, the number of *capite censi* in Rome immediately before the tribunate of Tiberius Gracchus could not have been large, both because unemployment had existed for only a few years previously and because the minimum of 4,000 *asses* was very low, it can be inferred that the manpower potential at Rome and throughout Italy for the purposes of recruitment for the legions was considerably greater than the number of enlisted soldiers. And if, as I believe, the *capite censi* were not included in

(129) *It. Bund*, p. 128.
(130) *Op. cit.*, p. 17.
(131) Livius, XXXI, 4, 1-2.
(132) Brunt, *op. cit.*, p. 366 ff.

the census figure, they amounted to 317,933 men on the eve of Tiberius Gracchus' tribuneship, in accordance with the figures of the census held in 136/5 B.C.

d) Conclusions

It can be asserted that the number of *assidui* was considerable since about one hundred settlements of Roman citizens were scattered throughout Italy (133), there were large reservoirs of citizens in the north, the centre and Campania, dispossession began on a massive scale only in the middle of the second century B.C., and the formation of the class of *capite censi* was accelerated only after 140 B.C. as a result of unemployment in Rome. Furthermore, there is no evidence that the problems of recruitment were due to a shortage of men, apart from the times of plague between 181 and 174 B.C. (134), while there is evidence that men were unwilling to join the army. Even if it is assumed that the *capite censi* were included in the census figures, the fact that in 70 B.C. cheap wheat was distributed to only 40,000 men indicates that, prior to Tiberius Gracchus' appearance on the political scene, the number of *capite censi* was small. The fact that the *capite censi* were included in the census figures has by no means been proved ; on the contrary, there are sound reasons for assuming that the opposite was true. Thus, even if the *capite censi* were included in the census figures, they accounted for only a small part of them, while the *assidui* constituted the vast majority. Although it is true that there were indications of a tendency not to have children, prior to Tiberius Gracchus' tribuneship this phenomenon was in its initial stages, and it cannot be supposed that it became a national scourge within a short time.

The foregoing makes it apparent that the problem of recruitment was by no means a juridical-demographic one, i.e. that there was a shortage of men who could legally be recruited to the legions, but rather one of politics, morale and bureaucracy, which came to a head during the war in Spain. The citizens did not want to join the army to be sent to Spain, because of the hardships of the war, the length of service, the minimal reward to be obtained, and the great likelihood of being killed or, at least, of losing one's property in Italy. On the other hand, the Senate was not

(133) Lily Ross Taylor, *The Voting Districts of the Roman Republic*, Rome, American Academy, 1960, p. 95 ff.

(134) Livius, XL, 19, 3 ; XLI, 21, 5.

firm in contending with this recalcitrance, perhaps because of a certain insensitivity, the desire to preserve tranquility in Rome and prevent tensions which could undermine its rule, and perhaps because of its awareness of the increasing political power of the masses, who were increasing in numbers at Rome and over whom its control was growing weaker. Indeed, it did not even carry out a reorganisation of recruitment methods, which would have enabled it to control the reserves of manpower at its disposal. Although Brunt rejects Polybius' statement that Rome was the only place where the inhabitants of the *ager Romanus* could be recruited, this rejection is based on grounds of logic alone and has no supporting evidence and, as is well known, rulers do not always act on the basis of logic. Elizabeth Rawson, on the other hand, accepts Polybius' statement ([135]). The system was far from perfect, in her opinion, and she asks : "Did the Romans never retain out-of-date and inefficient institutions?" She too discerned that the system enabled many not to report for recruitment.

The refusal of the populace to enlist, the Senate's weakness, and inefficient administration were the real reasons for the problems of recruitment which became acute on the eve of Tiberius Gracchus' tribuneship.

(135) *The Literary Sources for the Pre-Marian Army*, in *P.B.S.R.*, 1971, p. 15.

III

Tiberius Gracchus' Programme

a) The Propaganda of Tiberius Gracchus

At the beginning of his tribuneship, Tiberius Gracchus made a public speech in which he pointed out the problems facing Rome and put forward his solutions for them. The speech, which is quoted only by Appian (1), refers to the fact that the allies, who were valiant in war, were becoming impoverished and diminishing in number. It is also stated that the number of slaves, who did not serve in the army and were not faithful to their masters was increasing and constituted a danger. In order to bring home this point, Tiberius reminded his audience of the slave revolt in Sicily. He then proposed the agrarian law, within the framework of which land would be confiscated from the rich and distributed to the poor, *τοῖς πένησι*. There can, therefore, be no doubt that Tiberius presented the problem of the allies (2) and the threat to national security arising from the

(1) *B.C.*, 1, 3.

(2) On the fact that the *'Ιταλιῶται*, in Appian's account of Tiberius Gracchus, are only allies, see my article : *The Lex Agraria of 133 B.C. and the Italian Allies*, in *Athenaeum*, N.S. XLVIII (1970), p. 40 ff. There is no foundation for D. B. Nagle's claim (in *Athenaeum*, N.S. XLVIII [1970], p. 375 ff.) that Appian substituted the term 'Italian' for 'Roman', which he found in the sources used by him. Any assertion of this nature is pointless, since the sources in question have not been preserved. Furthermore, Nagle's argument is a weak one, being based on Appian's story that the allies were ruined by poverty, taxation and military service, even though in Nagle's opinion the allies did not pay taxes and the Romans did. The contrary, however, is true, since the allies paid taxes to their communities, while in 167 B.C. the *tributum*, i.e. the *εἰσφορά* mentioned by Appian which all Roman citizens had to pay, was no longer collected. Nagle's reasoning merely reinforces the view that the reference is to the allies, and his statement (*op. cit.*, p. 376, n. 15) that the Romans continued to complain about the taxes even after 167 B.C. is pure fabrication. Moreover, Nagle's interpretation of another passage in Appian (*B.C.*, I, 36) as indicating that the Italians had never been included among the recipients of *ager publicus* is essentially erroneous. True, in 91 B.C. some allies were apprehensive that land which they farmed would be taken away from them, since they had appropriated it illegally. But this land was described as *ἣν ἀνεμητὸν οὖσαν ἔτι*, i.e. it had not yet — *ἔτι* — been

large numbers of slaves to the Roman multitude. It seems highly probable that he connected the situation of the allies with the question of Rome's safety, although this is not stated explicitly in the speech cited by Appian. The reasons for making this assumption are as follows : a) In describing the background to Tiberius Gracchus' appearance Appian repeatedly stressed the fact that, as a result of the decline of the allies, a military-security problem had arisen. It can hardly be supposed that the historian would have phrased the background description, which forms a kind of prologue to the Tribuneship of 133 B.C., in this way, had it not been a vital aspect of Tiberius' reform, shedding light on the problems of the period as they were understood by him. b) Appian found it necessary to state that, in complaining about the bitter fate of the allies, Tiberius referred to them as extremely brave soldiers — *ἐσεμνολόγησε περὶ τοῦ Ἰταλικοῦ γένους ὡς εὐπολεμωτάτου*. Appian's use of the adjective *εὐπολεμωτατός* suggests that it was because they were brave fighters that their declining numbers disturbed Tiberius. This interpretation accords with the background description. c) It would have been pointless for Tiberius to address the Roman citizens at the beginning of his term of office, speaking at length about the tribulations of the allies and proffering a solution, without making it clear that the distress of the allies would also have an adverse effect on the Roman people. A purely benevolent concern for the allies was far removed from the minds of the citizens and Tiberius would have failed to make his point had he made a speech along these lines. It is, accordingly, almost certain that Tiberius' speech was in harmony with the tenor of the background description — namely, that the number of allies was shrinking and that the number of soldiers who could be recruited from their ranks was also declining. Consequently, measures would have to be taken which would increase their numbers, enabling more soldiers to be enlisted from among them.

On the other hand, it is unreasonable to suppose that Tiberius made no reference to the problems of the Roman citizens since, after presenting the contents of the speech, Appian reports that it roused partisan passion in Rome, among both the wealthy landowners and the poor, splitting the city into two conflicting camps (3). The speech produced a ferment in the

distributed. Then what about the land which had already been parcelled out? Was this not distributed to the allies either? Obviously, this phrase does not contradict the passage in Appian, *B.C.*, I, 7, where it is stated that land was divided up among the allies. Regarding the distribution of land to the allies see my article, *op. cit.*, p. 33, n. 28.

(3) *B.C.*, I, 10.

Roman multitude, and obviously referred to their harsh lot. The claims made against the rich by the poor also indicate the contents of the speech. They complained that they had been impoverished and were consequently unable to raise children. They mentioned the various wars in which they had participated to conquer Italy and grumbled at the fact that they had been deprived of their share of public property. Finally, they accused the wealthy of using slaves instead of employing freemen, citizens and soldiers.

It is quite obvious that the masses were not capable of putting forward these claims, or at least some of them, of its own accord, and that they were the outcome of propaganda. The first assertion is greatly exaggerated, since a small farmer was by no means a rich man. It is reasonable to assume, therefore, that the contention that they had formerly been rich but had become poor, a claim which is pure demagogy, was included in the speech in order to provoke the common people by contrasting the differences between their previous and present situations, thus aggravating their frustration and anger. Their claim that they had fought for the conquest of Italy was made one hundred and thirty years after the campaigns and two generations after the conclusion of the Hannibalic war. Obviously, among those who made these statements there was no one who remembered the war. The ignorant populace had no awareness of its own history, and if some of their number referred to events from the distant past, this was manifestly a repetition of propaganda made by people with a knowledge of history. An echo of this claim is to be found in Tiberius' second speech, an excerpt from which is quoted by Plutarch (4) : "But the men who fought for Italy have nothing except air and light." *Τοῖς δὲ ὑπὲρ τῆς 'Ιταλίας μαχομένοις καὶ ἀποθνήσκουσιν ἀέρος καὶ φωτός ἄλλου δὲ οὐδενὸς μέτεστιν.*

Evidently, at least some of the claims made by the masses, if not all of them, were stated in Tiberius' speech and it was this that caused the ferment amongst them. Appian adds that during the period of conflict between the two camps, a large number of people thronged into the city, joining one side or the other. These people were : *ἐν ταῖς ἀποίκοις πόλεσιν ἢ ταῖς ἰσοπολίτισιν ἢ ἄλλως ἐκοινώνει τῆσδε τῆς γῆς*. This makes it probable that Tiberius' speech also aroused great interest among the allies, who flocked to the city (5).

(4) *Tib. Gracch.*, 9.

(5) For the contention that the reference is to the allies, see : E. Gabba, *Appiani Bellorum Civilium, Liber Primus*, Firenze, 1958, p. 29 ; M. Gelzer, *K. Schr.*, 2, p. 92. The

Thus, Tiberius gave expression to problems affecting both the Roman citizens and the allies, and suggested solutions for them. The populace's immense enthusiasm after hearing the speech indicates that the solutions pleased them. Tiberius' mention of the plight of the allies in his first speech, their flocking into the city, and their joining the camp of the poor, clearly indicate that the proposed solution included distributing land to them too (6). This raises to the question, why did the Roman citizens consent to have partners in the distribution of land? What is still more surprising is that not only did they accept these associates, but they wanted the law to be passed at all costs (7) : *οἱ δ' ὡς κυρώσοντες ἐξ ἅπαντος*. Appian also reports that the suspense in anticipation of the day on which the law was to be passed was tremendous. The partnership did not constitute an obstacle, but appears to have been accepted willingly. How, then, did Tiberius succeed in persuading the Roman citizens to accept his plan? Without going into detail at this point, it can be said, in general terms, that Tiberius' speech stressed the fact that they were benefitting from the scheme and that the partnership with the allies was greatly to their advantage. Appian writes, however, that Tiberius' object was not to improve the economic situation of the poor, but to increase the number of men available for military service : *Γράκχῳ δ' ὁ μὲν νοῦς τοῦ βουλεύματος ἦν*

question is, why were the allies interested that this legislation should be passed? First and foremost, it should be stressed that not all the allies supported it, as is proved by the fact that some of them joined those who opposed it ; nor is there any evidence that these latter were confined to the rich, who feared that their land would be sequestered. It is possible, therefore, that some of those who opposed the legislation did so for other reasons, such as the fact that it imposed the greater burden of military service on them. As for those who supported the legislation, they may have been unaware of the increased obligation to serve in the army which it involved. It is reasonable to suppose that the rumours which spread through Italy concerning the proposed agrarian legislation focused on the distribution of land rather than on recruitment to the army. However, even if the opposite is assumed, namely, that the allies were aware of the law's military implications, there were still other reasons for their flocking to Rome. It is clear that only a small portion of the allies made their way to Rome, though it is not known from which places they came. The population of certain areas may have dwindled considerably, so that in these places support for the legislation was regarded as the lesser evil, at least easing the difficult economic situation. The law may also have been favoured by those who had already completed their quota of military service and consequently could only benefit from it. Again, men who would have had to join the army whatever happened may also have stood to gain by supporting Tiberius Gracchus. Thus, it is not difficult to explain why, despite that the agrarian law involved an increase in the military burden on the allies, there were those among them who flocked to Rome in order to support Tiberius Gracchus.

(6) See note 4 to the introduction of this book.

(7) *B.C.*, I, 10.

οὐκ ἐς εὐπορίας ἀλλὰ ἐς εὐανδρίαν (8). This indicates that Tiberius' overriding concern was for the state rather than for the poor of Rome. However, if Tiberius' propaganda was made in this spirit, the enthusiasm of the Roman multitude for the proposed law is incomprehensible, since the proposal implied that recipients of land would have to commit themselves to military service in return, a duty which the citizens did not like. It seems possible, therefore, that the statement that Tiberius' objective was not to improve the economic situation of the masses, but to increase the numbers of men eligible for military service does not reflect the spirit of the speech he made to the citizens of Rome. Consequently, the following possibilities have to be considered : a) The statement is perfectly correct, but Tiberius managed to conceal his true intentions in his speech. He presented the reform as a solution to the difficult economic situation of the poor citizens, while his real purpose was to recruit them for the army. In other words, his speech was simply deceit on a large scale. b) Appian was mistaken and misconstrued Tiberius' aim, which was restricted to the socio-economic, rather than to the military sphere. c) Tiberius' objectives was correctly understood by Appian, but only in part. Which, then, of these three possibilities is the most reasonable?

The answer is to be found in Tiberius' second speech, quoted by Appian (9), which he made when he was about to submit the proposed legislation to the approval of the Popular Assembly. Appian says that Tiberius brought forward new arguments in his speech, but does not claim that he presented any new proposals in addition to those already made public. Appian reports the contents of the speech as follows : To begin with, Tiberius asked several rhetorical questions, such as, Is it not right that the people should distribute public property amongst themselves? Does not a citizen deserve greater consideration than a slave? Is not a man who serves in the army more useful than one who does not? And should not someone who has a share in the public property pay greater attention to the needs of the public? These questions, then, make mention of the populace, the citizen, the soldier, and the individual who has a share in public property, but the allies are not referred to explicitly. The general tone is an appeal to justice, on the one hand, and to expediency on the other. An ethical attitude is adopted with regard to the citizen, who by his very position deserves greater consideration than a

(8) *B.C.*, I, 11.
(9) *B.C.*, I, 11.

slave, and justice demands that the people — the reference is obviously to those who vote in the popular assembly, i.e. the Roman citizens — should have a share in the public property. On the other hand, it is said that the soldier should be helped, because he is more useful than the individual who does not serve in the army, but it is not made clear whether the citizen and the soldier are one and the same. It is well-known that the allies also provided soldiers. Finally, the point is made that someone who has a share in public property will pay greater attention to public affairs, and here, too, it is not clear to whom reference is being made, whether to the citizens or the allies, nor is the manner in which this concern should be manifested explained. Thus, in the first part of the speech references are made to justice and expediency, and to citizens and those who are not citizens. The citizens are apparently intended to enjoy justice, but from whom the benefit will be derived, whether from the citizens or the allies, or both, is not made clear. If we consider Tiberius' first speech, in which he complained of the bitter lot of the allies, who were such valiant warriors, it is very probable that it was to them that he was referring when he put his rhetorical question whether the individual who had a share in public property would not benefit society as a whole.

Having posed these rhetorical questions, Tiberius warned his audience of the grave dangers facing Rome. The dilemma facing the State was whether the Romans would conquer the rest of the world by raising large numbers of brave men, or whether, because of their weakness and mutual jealousy, the enemy would regain from them what they had conquered so far. He then made his proposals, and attempted to convince the wealthy by telling them that, in order to realize their hopes, they should give the land as a gift to those who would rear children; he then outlined his suggestion once again. Finally, Appian reports, he continued to arouse the emotions of the masses on the one hand, and to appeal to the reason of the wealthy rather than to their desire for profit, on the other.

From Appian's account of the speech, it becomes clear that Tiberius addressed himself to the poor who had gathered in the popular assembly and carried them away by stressing the justice of their cause, their rights and the benefit to be gained by them. He also appealed to people's reason, emphasising the fact that the reform was essential for the State. This appeal was directed towards the wealthy, who would lose land, but by no means to them alone. At this point the question which arises is, how did Tiberius manage to combine the interests of the poor with the welfare of the State? In other words, how could he reconcile the State's need for many soldiers with the Roman citizens' disinclination to join the army?

(This disinclination has been discussed in the previous chapter.) It is perfectly evident that the security issue was stressed in the speeches, attention being focussed on the problem of the shortage of fighting men, and that the audience was well aware of the need for many soldiers. Thus, when Appian maintained that Tiberius' aim was to increase military manpower (and not to improve the economic situation of the poor) he had partially understood his objectives but had not grasped them in full. How, then, did Tiberius manage to carry the crowd away? If he had told the poor that they deserved land and that in the name of justice he wanted to distribute it to them, adding that this would also benefit the State since those who received land would join the army, it is doubtful whether, in view of their aversion to military service, the citizens would have followed him so devotedly and enthusiastically. It is evident that Tiberius made no attempt to mislead the multitude, since he explicitly mentioned the shortage of soldiers. Moreover, if Appian really did insert into the speech points which had not been made by Tiberius, and Tiberius had in effect attempted to mislead the crowd, he would have provided the wealthy with a powerful weapon for alienating the voters from him. True, they did conduct a propaganda campaign against him among the populace before the law was passed ; but all that is known of this is that they claimed that the reform would cause internal friction and destroy the regime [10], and not that it would harm the poor themselves. We know of no attempt to deter the crowd by the contention that the reform would do them more harm than good.

How, then, is it possible to explain the fact that, even though Tiberius laid great stress on the need to increase the number of soldiers, the masses supported him wholeheartedly and eagerly awaited the day on which the proposal would become law ?

As has been stated above, Tiberius discussed the situation of the citizens and the allies. In his first speech he emphasised his concern for the allies, apparently because of their military importance. In his second speech he stressed the citizens' right to a share in public property and the benefit which would be gained by the State, if an element of the population not classed in any category of citizenship but rather as 'soldiers' were also to profit through this. Thus, if the contents of the first speech are taken together with those of the second, it becomes apparent that, in stating that there were men to whom it would be worthwhile to distribute land,

(10) PLUT., *Tib.*, 9.

Tiberius was referring primarily to the allies. Consequently, whereas in his speeches Tiberius suggested distributing land to Roman citizens in the name of justice, with the object of improving their economic situation, he justified the division of land to the allies by claiming that this would increase their share of military service. He thus proposed a way of reducing the future military burden on the Roman citizens, and this accounts for their enthusiasm. They would benefit both economically and militarily and could hardly have hoped for a more attractive proposal.

In his proposed law Tiberius could have appealed to the reason of the wealthy by the following arguments : The suggested distribution of land would solve the problem of recruiting men for the Roman army. Since the Senate encountered difficulties in compelling citizens to enlist in the army, it was necessary to increase the burden borne by the allies. However, it was impossible to distribute land to the allies alone, since the citizens would not give their approval to legislation of this nature, and the land would, therefore, have to be distributed to the citizens too.

The course of events indicates that, until the law was approved, the multitude supported Tiberius wholeheartedly. They approved of his deposition of the Tribune Octavius and endorsed the legislation by a large majority. Tiberius' popularity reached its peak at the time when the law was passed (11), *Γράκχος δὲ μεγαλαυχούμενος ἐπὶ τῷ νόμῳ*, and he was accompanied to his home by the crowd as if he were the founder not merely of one city or race, but of all the Italian peoples (12). Undoubtedly, the voters were completely satisfied by the law, and there was no discrepancy between Tiberius' words and the clauses of the law itself. This absolute satisfaction was apparently due to the Roman citizens' awareness of the fact that, according to the law, they would benefit without having to pay in return for the lands they received. In addition it was likely that the duty of enlistment, which was resented by them, would be reduced, since the burden on the allies would be increased.

The Roman citizens might have approved Tiberius' agrarian law, even had they known that it compelled them to serve in the army. It is very doubtful, however, whether their enthusiasm would then have been so unbounded. However, even if the Roman citizens were capable of being enthusiastic over the distribution of land, regardless of its connection with military service, an examination of Tiberius' laws shows that the

(11) App., *B.C.*, I, 13.
(12) App., *B.C.*, I, 13.

distribution of land among the Roman citizens was carried out not in order to enlist them as soldiers, but so as to solve a social problem.

b) Tiberius Gracchus' Legislation

There can be little doubt that Tiberius Gracchus was the initiator and prime formulator of his own reforming legislation. However, since his supporters included men of outstanding talents and political power, including the two greatest jurists of the age, Licinius Crassus, Mucius Scaevola and the *princeps senatus* Appius Claudius, it is almost certain that this legislation was drawn up in consultation with these and other men. It seems unlikely that they would be satisfied with merely drawing up the final form of the law or with raising relevant legal points, and they must have influenced Tiberius to accept their opinions on matters of principle. It can be assumed that, during the preparations for getting the law passed, they engaged in an analysis of the existing situation and in evaluations of the nature of a solution to the ills of the society in which they live [13]. As stated above, among Tiberius' associates was Appius Claudius, the man who in 140 B.C. had passed the law forbidding recruitment twice in one year [14]. He could therefore have made it plain to Tiberius that the military problem was basically one of morale, and that the difficulties in raising troops were primarily due to the Roman citizens' lack of enthusiasm for serving in the army. Tiberius, for his part, could have reached a similar conclusion from what he saw with his own eyes during his military service in Spain. If the foregoing are assumptions, albeit reasonable ones, Tiberius' legislation gives us a surer picture of his concept of the situation and his objectives in introducing the reforms.

When Tiberius realised that, as a result of Octavius' deposition, he no longer stood on firm ground and his friends became aware of the conspiracy being formed against him, he attempted to extricate himself from his difficult situation by putting forward his candidacy for another term as Tribune. In order to win over the people he passed several laws, one of which reduced the length of military service [15]. Thus, if, when in

(13) For the view that the role played by the *patres* who supported the legislation was decisive, see : J. Carcopino, *La République de 133 à 44 avant J.-C.*, in *Histoire romaine*, Paris, 1935, Vol. II, p. 179 ff. There is, however, no evidence to support this. At any rate, this opinion simply upholds my conjecture that Tiberius was well aware of the problems of his period.

(14) Livius, *Epit.*, LIV.

(15) Plut., *Tib.*, 16. There is no evidence or reason for the assumption that the law

danger, Tiberius saw fit to introduce legislation of this nature, this indicates clearly that he knew that military service was distasteful to the masses, since he hoped to gain its support by reducing it. This fact supports the analysis given above, that it is hardly conceivable that in his propaganda he offered the citizens land in return for military service and at the same time gained their unconditional and enthusiastic support.

The law itself also indicates that Tiberius did not consider the root of the difficulties in the recruitment of citizens to be demographic. If his intention had been to tackle with the shortage of *assidui* by means of his agrarian legislation, the later law would have set it at naught. There is no need to stress the point that the reduction in the number of years served made it necessary to recruit more men. While it is possible that, finding himself in dire straits, Tiberius was prepared to disown his own policy and undermine the solution that he himself had proposed, it nevertheless seems highly unlikely, from the account of his character presented by the ancient sources, that he would have done anything of this sort. In comparing Agis and Cleomenes with the Gracchi, Plutarch depicts Tiberius as a noble man with the highest moral standards. He writes [16] : "No one dared say of the Gracchi, even those who spoke against them and hated them, that they were not innately superior in character to all other Romans or that they had not been superbly educated". Elsewhere he writes [17] : "But if it is necessary for me to express my opinion of one of them in particular, I would say that for personal excellence Tiberius was the foremost". Velleius Paterculus also extols Tiberius' virtues, describing him as a superior man. He writes [18] : *Vir alioqui uita innocentissimus ingenio florentissimus proposito sanctissimus tantis denique adornatus uirtutibus quantas perfecta et natura et industria mortalis condicio recipit.*

It seems highly unlikely that someone whose character and personal qualities were so highly praised and who had proved his courageous spirit by the revolutionary fervour of his conduct on the stage of history, would so reduce himself in stature as to be prepared, in effect, to disown his whole struggle and policy. In short, the law under discussion indicates that Tiberius was fully aware of the fact that the populace sought to avoid

was passed by Gaius, as maintained by EARL, *op. cit.*, p. 38, and SMITH, *Service in the Post Marian Roman Army*, p. 8, n. 3. In referring to this legislation, LAST states, in *C.A.H.*, Vol. VIII, p. 32 : "The programme is one which cannot with confidence be rejected, the need for some change in regulations for military service was already acute".

(16) *Agis and Cleomenes and the Gracchi*, 1.

(17) *Op. cit.*, 5.

(18) VELL. PATERC., II, 2, 2.

military service, regarding it as a burden. It was also apparent to him that the recruitment problems were not due to a lack of men who could be enlisted by law, i.e. to a shortage of *assidui*.

Again, the agrarian law itself makes it clear that Tiberius' aim was not to increase the number of citizens who could be recruited legally, nor did it constitute an attempt to encourage the Roman peasant to join the army. The *lex agraria* of 111 B.C. shows that the land which was distributed to the poor under Tiberius' agrarian law did not fall into the category of *censui censendo*, i.e. during the census it was not registered by the censors as being the property of the person who received it [(19)]. *Capite censi* who received land under the terms of Tiberius' agrarian law did not, therefore, become *assidui* as a result. In other words, the recipient of land did not become liable to recruitment as a result of having acquired land. It seems reasonable to assume that this legal fact did not escape Tiberius, and there can be no shadow of a doubt that his associates, the prominent jurists, were fully aware of it. Had the legislators' intention been to create additional citizens who were liable for military service, such outstanding jurists as Crassus and Scaevola would undoubtedly have found a way of expressing this in the actual text of the law.

While it may be that, for tactical reasons, in order to prevent the multitude from becoming suspicious and so as to gain their support, the law was phrased as it was, its underlying intention was, in time, to turn the land-recipients, through their yields, into *assidui*, consequently making them liable for military service. This possibility seems slight, since the law contained a clause which made no contribution to the objective of recruiting men, and which served solely to heighten the disinclination to serve in the army. As is known, the law contained a paragraph prohibiting recipients of land from selling it. This meant that there was no possibility of restoring the land if it was ruined as a result of the farmer's long absence due to military service. If a farmer was unable to sell his land or transfer it to someone else, being entitled only to bequeath it to his family, he was prevented from mortgaging it in order to borrow funds for its restoration. If a small farmer of this kind were recruited into the army it would be absolutely clear to him that he faced total ruin and that military service meant his destruction as a farmer. It seems highly improbable that this fact escaped the notice of Tiberius and his associates or that they did not realize that the law was potentially destructive to the

(19) L, 8.

solutions it proferred, if its aim was to increase the number of citizens obliged to serve in the army. Moreover, Tiberius, as already stated, was aware that the problems of recruitment stemmed from the citizens' unwillingness to serve in the army. The agrarian law would not alter this situation. On the contrary, a farmer who knew that his military service would lead to the ruin of his farm and that there would be very little possibility of his being able to rehabilitate it, except by obtaining plunder from a rich enemy, would develop an ever-increasing resistance to recruitment. Thus, the legislation added another dimension to the disinclination to join the army.

This being so, and since it is absolutely clear that Tiberius' objective was to increase the number of soldiers in the Roman army, the only logical solution was to increase the number of soldiers recruited from among the allies (and not to impose any additional burden on the Roman citizens). An item of information recorded by Velleius Paterculus supports this contention. He states that Tiberius proposed that Roman citizenship should be granted to all the inhabitants of Italy ([20]). This information has been considered incorrect ([21]), but from Tiberius' viewpoint it was an extremely reasonable step. Until Tiberius Gracchus' time the proportion of allies and Roman citizens recruited into the army had been 1 : 1, approximately (see the following section of this chapter). The population ratio according to Polybius' manpower assessment of 225 was 2 : 1. From census figures dating from the end of the second century B.C. and from the census of 70/69 it can be deduced that this proportion remained more or less constant ([22]). Tiberius' proposal to grant citizenship to the allies (if Velleius was right) involved doubling the burden of recruitment on them. Their obligations were made equal to those of the established Roman citizens, without their being able to complain of discrimination and injustice. In this way, the number of soldiers joining the army would increase, while the burden of recruitment on established Roman citizens would remain unchanged or even decline.

(20) II, 1, 2.

(21) Earl, *op. cit.*, p. 113 ; Badian, in *F.C.*, p. 170, n. 2.

(22) The census figure for 115/4 was 394,336. If as a result of the heavy losses incurred at the battle of Arausio and in the war with the allies, the number of citizens was reduced by only 50,000 (the losses recorded in the sources are far higher than this), after the war with the allies the established citizens numbered 348,000. If it is taken into account that the census figure for 70/69 B.C., which was 910,000, was a partial one, since thousands of soldiers outside Italy and many allies were not included, the figure was at least double that of the established citizens.

Thus, when Tiberius proposed, in a moment of personal crisis, to reduce the number of years Roman citizens served in the army, he was not proposing anything opposed to his basic aim and intentions. He was aware that the question of recruitment was an involved one, and since he was dependent upon the multitude he did not clash with them on this issue, but tried to solve the problem in another way. Moreover, like Appius Claudius, Tiberius made an effort to accommodate the populace, and whereas his agrarian law was not intended to make the burden of recruitment more severe for them, his later legislation actually lightened it.

The agrarian law makes it clear that, in granting land to the poor among the Roman citizens, Tiberius sought to rehabilitate the class of the small farmers, which had been reduced to ruin. His object in so doing was not to provide a source of recruits, but to revive ancient Roman society and to prevent the creation of an unemployed Roman proletariat, with its potentially destructive effects.

c) Recruitment among the Allies from the Second Punic War until the War of the Marsi

The ancient sources give the following accounts of the contribution of the allies to the Roman army: Appian states that during the Second Punic War the allies provided twice as many soldiers as the citizens (23). Polybius reports that, during his lifetime, their numbers in the Roman infantry was equal to those of the Roman citizens (24). Velleius reports the allies claim that, although they provided twice the number of soldiers for the Roman army, they were not granted citizenship, and that this was the reason for the outbreak of the War of the Allies (25).

Thus, according to the sources, after the Second Punic War the proportion of allies in the ranks of the Roman army declined, increasing once again around the year 90 B.C. Modern scholarship indicates that although this picture is not precise, it is correct in a general sense. Indeed, Brunt reaches the conclusion (26) that from the beginning of the Second Punic War until the Battle of Cannae the ratio was two soldiers from

(23) *Bell. Hann.*, 8.

(24) VI, 26, 7 ; VI, 30, 2. The number of infantry was equal. The number of cavalry from among the allies was three times as large. The ratio was, therefore, 1 : 1,1.

(25) II, 15, 1.

(26) *Italian Manpower*, p. 679 ff.

among the allies to each one from among the Roman citizens. But after this battle, and throughout the rest of the war, the ratio was 1 : 1. This indicates that Appian was in error, even though immediately after the war the ratio was again two soldiers from the allies to one Roman, and this was maintained more or less until 180 B.C. Afterwards it was approximately 1 : 1 (27). Thus, Polybius' assertion is generally correct for the period between 180 or thereabouts and the end of the second third of the century. However, the extant numerical information, which refers to a later period, shows that the burden on the allies was doubled. In both the Jugurtha War and the battle of Arausio the ratio was two soldiers from the allies to every soldier who was a Roman citizen (28). From this it can be inferred that the claims made by the allies regarding their contribution to the Roman army, as reported by Velleius, were most probably correct. A very significant point in the present context is that the assertions made by the ancient sources and the numerical data both indicate that, after the year 133 B.C., the proportion of the allies in the army increased (29). The question then arises whether this growth was connected with Tiberius Gracchus' proposal. Before answering this question, an attempt will be made to answer another, namely, why did the proportion of allies in the Roman army decline from approximately 2 : 1 at the beginning of the second century to approximately 1 : 1 later on during the same century ? The answer to this second question will be of assistance to us in attempting to answer the first one.

There is not much data available for answering this question, but there are several events which shed some light on what occurred. In his description of the background to Tiberius Gracchus' appearance upon

(27) BRUNT, *op. cit.*, p. 681 ; TOYNBEE, *op. cit.*, II, p. 128 ff.

(28) BRUNT, *op. cit.*, p. 685.

(29) BRUNT, *op. cit.*, pp. 685-686. Concerning the allies in the Roman army during this period, see : E. GABBA, in *Athenaeum*, XXIX, 1951, p. 190, n. 2. On the basis of APP., *Ill.*, 10, Brunt concludes that the ratio was maintained still in 135 B.C. This passage reports that the consul in that year, Fulvius Flaccus, had at his disposal a large force of 10,000 infantry and 600 cavalry. In Brunt's opinion the reference is to a legion and an auxiliary force of equal size. Although this interpretation cannot be dismissed, it can equally be maintained that this force comprised two legions, without any auxiliary force. It is known that the consular *imperium* consisted of two legions and the number of cavalry cited accords with the number serving in two legions, 300 in each legion. Polybius, however, reports that the number of cavalry provided by the allies was three times as large as that provided by the Roman citizens (see *supra*, note 24). Consequently, it is to be assumed that the cavalry of the legion and its accompanying auxiliary force amounted to 1,200 men, and not 600.

the political scene, Appian states that, as a result of the process of dispossession, the allies were so impoverished and diminished in number that there was concern at Rome that their numbers would not suffice for recruitment to the army. As was stated in the previous chapter, it seems doubtful whether the allies were in fact numerically reduced, but it is reasonable to suppose that they conducted propaganda along these lines in Rome, with the intention of reducing their enlistment quota. The fact that propaganda of this kind was indeed conducted can be learned from Appian and Plutarch (see pp. 47-49). There were several incidents to indicate that the allies claimed that they suffered from a shortage of manpower. During the Second Punic War, in 209, twelve Latin colonies maintained that they were unable to provide Rome with soldiers, since their numbers had been severely diminished [30]. When, several years later, they were punished for their recalcitrance by being obliged to raise twice as many soldiers as the maximum number mobilised by them during one year of the Second Punic War, they protested vehemently that this was not within their power. After pressure had been exerted and threats made, it transpired that the colonies could do as they had been ordered [31]. There are two well-known passages in Livy which deal with the complaints made by Latin and non-Latin allies to the Roman Senate concerning their declining population. The first passage [32] contains no reference to the question of recruitment; but in the second, which concerns the year 177 B.C., we find the following : "The delegations of Latin allies also shocked the Senate. They had already wearied the previous Censors and Consuls. Their principal claim was that many of their citizens had been rated at Rome and had emigrated to settle there. Should this be permitted in future, within a few decades their cities would be desolate and their forsaken fields unable to contribute a single soldier. The delegates of the Samnites and the Faelignians claimed that about 4000 families had emigrated to Fregellae, but that the quota of soldiers they were compelled to raise had not been reduced" [33].

Apart from this piece of information, there is other evidence of the colonies' difficulties. In the year 200 B.C. a commission of three men was established in order to make up the quota of settlers at Venusia, which had suffered during the Hannibalic war. The commission sent new settlers to

(30) Livius, XXVII, 9.
(31) Livius, XXIX, 15.
(32) Livius, XXXIX, 3.
(33) Livius, XXXI, 8-9.

this colony (34). In 199 B.C. Narnia asked the Senate for additional settlers, claiming that the number of its inhabitants had not reached the figure fixed at its establishment. An investigatory committee which examined this contention found it correct, and the Senate permitted new settlers to be sent (35). A similar claim made by Cosa in the same year was rejected (36), but two years later the colony received one thousand new settlers (37). In 190 Cremona and Placentia received new settlers (38), as did Cales in 184 (39). Although the difficult situation of these colonies was a result of the Second Punic War and of hostilities which occurred shortly after its conclusion, rather than of the socio-economic process which affected Italy during the second century B.C., these passages do indicate that claims were made concerning the lack of manpower in the colonies and that the Senate recognised their validity.

When we piece together the various pieces of evidence they provide the following general picture. As early as during the Second Punic War some of the Latin allies complained of shortage of manpower and maintained that they were unable to provide soldiers for the Roman army. After the conclusion of the war, colonies continued to complain of diminishing numbers, and this was found by the Senate to be justified. Claims of this kind appear to have increased during the second and third decades of the second century B.C. as a result of a movement of population, and they were also recognised by the Senate (40), which ordered allies who had settled in Rome to return to their birthplaces. From Appian and Plutarch we learn that, just before Tiberius' appearance, these complaints were intensified and the impression received in Rome was that the entire population of Italy was contracting rapidly.

The increased proportion of allies in the ranks of the Roman army immediately after the Second Punic War may have been due to the Roman nation's weariness of the burden of war. This was reflected quite

(34) Livius, XXXI, 49.

(35) Livius, XXXII, 2.

(36) Livius, XXXII, 2.

(37) Livius, XXXIII, 24.

(38) Livius, XXXVII, 46.

(39) *C.I.L.*, I, p. 200, no. 32. J. S. Reid, *Problems of the Second Punic War*, in *J.R.S.*, V (1915), p. 121 ; Salmon, in *J.R.S.*, XXVI (1936), p. 57.

(40) Afzelius, *Die römische Kriegsmacht während der Auseinandersetzung mit der hellenistischen Grossmächtigen*, Copenhagen, 1944, p. 13. This author claims that in 169 B.C. the number of Latins was greater than in 225 B.C. while the number of non-Latin allies was smaller.

clearly in their lack of enthusiasm for starting the Second Macedonian War, and also in their anger against the allies who either turned traitor during the course of the war, going over to Hannibal's side, or refused to cooperate with Rome. The reduction of the burden around the year 180 B.C. can be explained by the abating of the animosity towards the allies, and also by the presures and claims which have been discussed above. The Senate, which recognised the validity of the claims made, may consequently have agreed to reduce the quota of soldiers, fixing it according to the ration recorded by Polybius.

Since the sources concerning the period after the Pydna War are extremely few, we have little information about the relations between Rome and her allies after this war and until the appearance of Tiberius Gracchus on the political scene. The only significant source is Appian, from whom we learn that the issue of recruitment to the army from among the allies had become acute. Possibly, during this period the allies' claims that the decline in their population prevented them from fulfilling their military obligations had become more frequent and more insistent. It may even be hypothesised that, from the middle of the second century, demands had been made on the allies to increase their quota of soldiers, as a result of the Roman citizens' unwillingness to serve in the army. The allies, for their part, may have reacted with the claim that the diminution of their population made it impossible for them to fulfil these demands. The Roman populace's fear of a decline in the number of the allies, as reported by Appian, may have reflected this situation. Tiberius Gracchus' task was, therefore, to cope with both the problem of recruitment and the allies' claims.

d) Conclusions

It is evident that, after the year 133 B.C., the proportion of the allies in the Roman army increased ; and from Tiberius Gracchus' propaganda it may be presumed that he cannot have proposed increasing the quota of soldiers raised from among the Roman citizens, but that the increase was to come from the ranks of the allies. Moreover, from his legislation it is highly improbable that he proposed to distribute land to the citizens in order to make them legally liable for recruitment. The conclusion to which this leads is that it was Tiberius who first formulated the policy of transferring most of the burden of enlistment onto the allies, in order to overcome the difficulties encountered in recruiting soldiers from among the citizens. However, being aware of their situation and, most probably, of their complaints, he included them among the recipients of land. He apparently hoped in this way to contend effectively with both their impoverished circumstances and their claims.

I have shown elsewhere [41] that, after Tiberius' death, his reform was implemented, not in accordance with his intentions but in the Senate's selfish interests. Land was sequestered primarily from the allies, it would seem, and distributed solely to the Roman citizens. As far as recruitment was concerned, the Senate took the easy and convenient course of adopting Tiberius Gracchus' policy and doubling the recruitment quota imposed on the allies [42] without, however, granting them the compensation laid down in the agrarian law. The Senate thought that the problem of recruitment could be solved without its having to contend with the Roman citizen body, or to make any sacrifices. It was, however, mistaken in this, and by its policy sowed the seeds of the antagonism between Rome and the allies.

Although some time previous to Tiberius' appearance the allies had already felt abused and discriminated against, Appian was right in connecting the beginnings of the real antagonism with the period after Tiberius' death. Nevertheless, he did not fully grasp all the component elements of the situation. The Senate then adopted a policy which adversely affected the allies as a body, not just as one city or another, as one military unit or as private individuals, but all the allies, rich and poor alike. Land was taken away from the wealthy, often arbitrarily, with no compensation being made ; and the military burden upon the poor was increased, without any commensurate recompense. The Senate's policy during the years following Tiberius' death of taking from the allies while giving them nothing in return, laid the basis for the conflict which erupted in the year 90 B.C.

(41) *Athenaeum*, N.S. XLVIII (1970), p. 42 ff.

(42) It does not mean that Tiberius decided to double the allies quota, although his policy was to make their burden heavier.

EPILOGUE

Tiberius Gracchus as a Statesman

Plutarch and Appian are the two major sources of information about Tiberius Gracchus' tribuneship and representing two different traditions, the one regarding him as a Roman social reformer and the other as a pan-Italic military reformer. The arguments presented in the previous chapter demonstrate that one version does not necessarily contradict the other, but rather that the two of them together give us the complete picture, viz. that Tiberius was both a Roman social and a pan-Italic military reformer. This view enables us to accept fragments of information which are in accordance with it but have been rejected by contemporary scholars, although no evidence to the contrary has been adduced. It also allows us to take Appian's account concerning the allies literally and to reject groundless attempts to amend it or attribute to it intentions which are not to be found in it. And, finally, this synoptic view permits us to judge Tiberius afresh as a statesman, assessing his influence on the course of Roman history from an angle which has been entirely overlooked by modern scholarship.

The accepted view regards Tiberius Gracchus as a reformer whose sphere of interest was limited to the Roman populace and who aspired to revive Roman society by refashioning it after the pattern of the first centuries of the Republic. This approach represents him, though not always explicitly, as a naive romantic who neither understood his era nor realised that the major changes which had occurred in Rome made it impossible to put the clock back. In so doing, it passes judgment not only on Tiberius Gracchus, but also on the senators who were his associates, men with a wealth of practical experience of Roman life and its problems. If this view is accepted, these respected senators must also be considered to have been naive dreamers, supporting the delusions and fantasies of a young man. It seems improbable that this was in fact the case. There is too great a discrepancy between the sophisticated efforts invested in the actual legislation — the manœuvring in order to make it appear non-revolutionary in character and in essence merely an updated version of an ancient law, the extreme consideration shown for the fellings of the aristocracy, which stood to lose most, in order to minimise the expected opposition — and the naivety of the law's objective as presented by modern scholarship. The law is too sophisticated for us to be able to believe that it was drawn up by small-minded, petty men.

Even those scholars who praise Tiberius Gracchus' personality against the background of contemporary Roman conservatism — and his audacity in striking at the "establishment" in an effort to bring about far-reaching changes may also misjudge him (perhaps unconsciously) as a statesman, when they accept the view that his aim was to revive the class of small farmers, the backbone of Roman society, so that in the course of time its members should serve as soldiers as well as farmers. Tiberius and his supporters would have had to be stupid in the extreme to fail to grasp the basic fact that for a farmer military service spelt ruin. They would also have had to be blind and deaf not to notice that the populace was trying to evade military service and that the army in Spain, of which Tiberius had first-hand knowledge, was in a state of demoralisation. How, then, could they have expected the redistribution of land to the citizens to increase the general willingness to fight, seeing that the farmers would once more have something to lose and would again face disaster. Tiberius was, after all, trying to bind the recipients of the plots and their land. This was surely the germ of the attempt to differentiate between farmer and soldier, which was later developed by Augustus. If a farmer were to serve in some distant place, the land would become barren and there would be no chance of revitalizing it without a renewed financial investment. Is it, therefore, conceivable that Tiberius wanted to revive traditional Roman agriculture in this way? Tiberius and his associates were far more sensible than that.

It is no coincidence that the impetus for the reform came from a man who had witnessed the humiliation of the Roman army, which was on the verge of annihilation in Spain. Undoubtedly, the traumatic experience Tiberius had undergone when he was trapped with the army had shocked him into a sense of impending disaster and into the conviction that matters could not continue as they were. He was one of the very few members of the aristocracy who were capable of uttering the assertion that Rome stood at a parting of the ways and must either continue to expand or degenerate and lose its conquests. It is hardly surprising that many senators were not much impressed by these sentiments, for Rome ruled the world, and they considered themselves its masters. Moreover, they knew that Rome's victories had begun with defeats and therefore the events in which Mancinus was involved did not constitute anything very exceptional. They also knew that the army in Spain was being led by Scipio, Rome's foremost commander, and that victory was at hand. But this was not how Tiberius saw matters. The sense of danger he felt led to his proposing a solution which left a deep mark on Roman history for hundreds of years.

Tiberius, it is true, did not attempt to offer the citizens incentives to enlist. He may well have regarded the lack of enthusiasm for military service as a basic feature of Roman society which it would be very difficult to change. There is an important difference between Tiberius Gracchus' policy and that of the great commanders of the first century B.C., who distributed land as a reward for military service. They granted the land after service, so there was no danger that the veterans would lose it in consequence of their service. Whereas Tiberius, it will be recalled, intended to bestow land on citizens without linking this to military service, and this would simply have heightened their unwillingness to join the army. On the other hand, Augustus, the great reorganiser who tackled the whole complex of the army's problems, did not stop at establishing a standing army governed by regulations regarding conditions of service, but also adopted Tiberius' way of thinking. In transferring a considerable part of the recruitment to Cisalpine Gaul he was following Tiberius' approach. He realised that economic guarantees for soldiers were not enough and that it was necessary to ease the burden on war-weary population by shifting the load onto a more vigorous sector of the population.

In striving at increasing the contribution of the allies to the Roman army, Tiberius created a pattern of political thought which prevailed at the close of the republic and throughout the Imperial period. The realization that one section of the population alone could not be expected to bear the burden continuously and that it should be distributed among other, new sections, had a far-reaching influence on the Roman Empire at a later date, but this is not the appropriate place to discuss this. Suffice it to mention a number of facts which prove that Tiberius' line of thought was firmly established for hundreds of years after his death. From his time onwards the number of allies in the army increased, as did that of the new citizens after the year 90. At any rate, during the first century B.C. not many soldiers were enlisted in Rome. Augustus began to ease the burden of recruitment on Republican Italy and enlisted many soldiers in Cisalpine Gaul. This trend was reinforced during the Julio-Claudian era, when the provinces were also included. In this period recruitment was limited in extent within Republican Italy, being concentrated on Cisalpine Gaul and also conducted in many other parts of the Empire. From Vespasian's time onwards the burden of recruitment on Cisalpine Gaul was eased considerably, the principal part of it being shifted to the provinces. Thus, the integration of the barbarians into the Roman army from the third century A.D. on was not a startling innovation, but simply the extention of a recruitment policy which had been in operation for hundreds of years.

It is not easy to judge Tiberius' policy. At first sight, it can be said that his solution was superficial and that he made no attempt to come to terms with the actual problem of unwillingness to join the army. However, if we take into account the fact that the population under discussion had been fighting continuously for about four hundred years, his solution of showing consideration for the Roman people was basically correct. He also showed vision in his treatment of the allies. He understood that they had to be made to feel that they were not merely an exploited sector of the population, but that there was someone in the Roman government who was concerned about their interests. If Velleius' report is correct and Tiberius proposed granting citizenship to all the inhabitants of Italy, his intention was not only to increase recruitment among them, but also to raise their motivation and accord them a heightened sense of sharing a common destiny.

Tiberius, then, was not a reformer whose proposed solutions left no trace behind, and whose historical importance lies only in the negative fact that he served as a catalyst for the beginning of a new period of internal struggles and social deterioration. Against the background of Roman conservatism and institutional inflexibility, he should be regarded as a bold revolutionary. Although he failed in his attempt to rehabilitate Roman society and to arrest the socio-economic process of sequestration and proletarization for reasons which were beyond his control, he did nevertheless succeed in leaving his mark on the sphere of military recruitment until the end of the Empire. He also initiated a new policy of consideration and rapprochement towards the allies which, because of the Senate's attitude, was implemented only after the bitter war of 90 B.C.